The Case for Multinational Federalism

Throughout the world, liberal democracies are grappling with increasing claims made in the name of minority national, socio-cultural and ethno-cultural identities that seek greater recognition in the institutions of the nation-state. This work inserts itself into debates centred on diversity through a normative and empirical analytical assessment of the political sociology of multinational democracies. The main thread of the arguments put forward is that federalism, in both its institutional manifestations and its sociological properties, constitutes a promising avenue for the management of cohabitating political communities and for the affirmation of collective identities within states that are constituted by two or more nations.

Author Alain-G. Gagnon develops his argument by contending that the federal principle allows for the exercise of advanced democratic practices within nation-states, permitting internal nations to openly affirm the bases of adherence to a common political project. At the same time, he argues that federalism nourishes the development of distinct collective traditions that serve to benefit all parties to the association. It is concluded that only in such a scenario will the elusive pursuit of an authentic and shared loyalty underpin multination states and ensure their stability, in contrast to the instrumental sentiments of belonging engendered by procedural territorial federal models.

Focusing primarily on the Canadian case, this book also draws inspiration from other federal states (Belgium, the United States), as well as federalizing states (Spain, the United Kingdom). It will be of keen interest to students and scholars of Politics, European Studies, along with Nationalism and Federalism Studies.

Alain-G. Gagnon holds the Canada Research Chair in Québec and Canadian Studies, is Director of the Centre de recherche interdisciplinaire sur la diversité au Québec (CRIDAQ,) and is a Professor in the Political Science Department at the Université du Québec à Montréal, Canada. He is also Director of the Research Group on Multinational Societies.

Routledge series in federal studies
(Formerly The Cass series in regional and federal studies)
ISSN 1363–5670

Edited by Michael Burgess
Centre for Federal Studies, University of Kent, UK
Formerly edited by John Loughlin
Cardiff University, UK

This series brings together some of the foremost academics and theorists to examine the timely subject of regional and federal studies, which since the mid-1980s have become key questions in political analysis and practice.

The Case for Multinational Federalism

Beyond the all-encompassing nation

Alain-G. Gagnon

Routledge
Taylor & Francis Group

LONDON AND NEW YORK

First published 2010
by Routledge
2 Park Square, Milton Park, Abingdon, Oxon OX14 4RN

Simultaneously published in the USA and Canada
by Routledge
711 Third Ave, New York, NY 10017

The original French edition of this book was published by the
Institut d'Estudis Autonomics, Generalitat de Catalunya, and was
awarded the *Prize Josep Maria Vilaseca I Marcet*.

Routledge is an imprint of the Taylor & Francis Group, an informa business

© 2010 Alain-G. Gagnon

First issued in paperback 2013

Typeset in Sabon by Wearset Ltd, Boldon, Tyne and Wear

British Library Cataloguing in Publication Data
A catalogue record for this book is available from the British Library

Library of Congress Cataloging in Publication Data
Gagnon, Alain.
The case for multinational federalism: beyond the all-encompassing
nation/Alain-G.Gagnon.
p. cm. – (Routledge series in federal studies; 18)
Includes bibliographical references and index.

1. Federal government. 2. Cultural pluralism. 3. Ethnicity–Political
aspects. 4. Nation-state. 5. Comparative government. I. Title.

JC355.G323 2009
320.4'049–dc22
2009007756

ISBN13: 978-0-415-54648-5 (hbk)
ISBN13: 978-0-415-85098-8 (pbk)

The author and publisher would like to draw attention to the fact that the original French edition of this book was published by the Institut d'Estudis Autonomics (Generalitat de Catalunya).

Contents

Illustrations

Figure

Table

Acknowledgements

I have wanted to write a book on "might makes right" or the duty to consider the multination for a long time. This book is intended for specialists, students, decision-makers and individuals seeking greater knowledge of the world around us. My experience in Canada has allowed me to take the pulse of two distinct traditions, and my experience on the international scene has expanded and deepened my knowledge by highlighting new traditions. Thus, James Bickerton, Alan C. Cairns, Maureen Covell, Francis Delpérée, Daniel Elazar, Donald Smiley, Ronald Watts and, among colleagues of my generation, Michael Burgess, Enric Fossas, Guy Laforest, Luis Moreno, Alain Noël, Patrick Peeters and Ferran Requejo have led me to study the federal approach in depth.

I feel I owe a major debt to many researchers and students with whom I have rubbed shoulders over the last 25 years. A number of research assistants contributed to the preparation of this book with respect to documentary research, bibliography preparation and proof-reading. I am especially grateful to Martine Boisvert, Olivier De Champlain, Bernard Gagnon, Raffaele Iacovino, Louiselle Lévesque, Charles-Antoine Sévigny and Pierre Skilling. For the English version of this book, I wish to thank Mary Baker who has translated large portions of the manuscript. The work of Marc Hanvelt, Carleton University (Ottawa), is also acknowledged at the final and crucial revision stage. A note of thanks goes to Carles Viver, Director of the Institut d'Estudis Autonomics, Generalitat de Catalunya, for his support and granting us the right to publish this work in English and to Michael Burgess for his encouragement during the preparation of this book.

Finally, the research in this book was supported by a Quebec Government subsidy under its support programme in the area of intergovernmental affairs and Quebec identity.

Note on the author

Alain-G. Gagnon holds the Canada Research Chair in Québec and Canadian Studies, is Director of the Centre de recherche interdisciplinaire sur la diversité au Québec (CRIDAQ,) and is a Professor in the Political Science Department at the Université du Québec à Montréal. He is also the Director and a founding member of the Groupe de recherche sur les sociétés plurinationales (Research Group on Multinational Societies) based at UQAM. In addition to teaching at Queen's, Carleton and McGill universities from 1982 to 2003, he has been a visiting professor at the Institut d'Études Politiques de Bordeaux, the Universidat autonoma de Barcelona and the Universitat Pompeu Fabra, as well as Senior Scholar at the Institute for Research on Public Policy in Montréal. Professor Gagnon also serves as Director of the *Débats* book collection at Éditions Québec Amérique, *Diversitas* collection with Peter Lang and of the *Trajectoires* collection at Boréal.

Professor Gagnon's works on political parties, identity, diversity, federalism and the multination have been translated into a dozen languages. He has published over 40 books, more than 100 scholarly articles and given over 200 conferences around the world. His publications include *Multinational Democracies* (Cambridge University Press, 2001) with James Tully, *Ties that Bind: Parties and Voters in Canada* (Oxford University Press, 2001) with James Bickerton, Munroe Eagles and Patrick Smith, *Québec: State and Society*, 3rd edition (University of Toronto Press, 2003), *Federalism, Citizenship, and Quebec* (University of Toronto Press, 2007) with Raffaele Iacovino, *Contemporary Canadian Federalism: Foundations, Traditions, Institutions* (University of Toronto Press, 2009) and *Cities Under Stress: Facing Cultural Diversity* (Presses Universitaires de Lyon, 2009) with Bernard Jouve. His forthcoming books include *Canadian Politics* (5th edition, University of Toronto Press) with James Bickerton and *Federal Democracies* (Routledge) with Michael Burgess.

He serves on the scientific committees of a number of scholarly journals, including *Cahiers de recherche sociologique, Politique et Sociétés, Quebec Studies, Regionalism and Federalism* and *Revista d'Estudis Autonomics i Federals*. In 2006, he received the Josep Maria Vilaseca I Marcet book award for *Au-delà de la nation unificatrice: plaidoyer pour le fédéralisme multinational* granted by the Centre d'Estudis Autonomics (Catalonia); followed in 2007 by the Marcel-Vincent Award, granted by the Association francophone pour l'avancement des sciences (Québec), paying tribute to Gagnon's lifetime academic achievements in the social sciences. In 2008, he was received by the Royal Society of Canada for his influential work on small nations as well as nations without states.

Introduction
The merits of federalism and new awareness of the multination

Throughout the world, liberal democracies are grappling with the growing salience of political cleavages that stem from claims, made in the name of minority national, socio-cultural and ethno-cultural identities, for greater recognition in the institutions of the nation-state. This work inserts itself into debates centred on diversity through a normative and empirical analytical assessment of the political sociology of multinational democracies and the institutional possibilities of federalism. The central argument is that federalism, in both its institutional manifestations and its sociological character-istics, constitutes a promising avenue for the management of cohabitating political communities and for the affirmation of collective identities within states that are constituted by two or more nations.

Federal institutions that respect the existence of a plurality of nations within a single state serve as a safeguard against the real or potential oppression of minority nations. Many thinkers in the tradition of liberal neutrality who espouse methodological individualism claim that the recognition of collective rights undermines the privileged place of equal citizenship and is thereby de-stabilizing to liberal democratic institutions. This book aims to show that, by disregarding the salient political cleavages that are unique to multination settings and by relying on majoritarian democratic institutions to settle political conflicts, many states in the contemporary era are actually perpetuating instability and denying legitimate democratic outcomes to political projects directed by majority nationalist sentiment. Indeed, institutions based on multinational federalism, open to deliberation and negotiation between collective groupings, are better suited to allow for the flourishing of a diversity of collective identities, including self-determining minority nations, and best serve the ends of justice and stability in the contemporary societies of liberal democracies that are characterized by diversity.

"Might makes right" explains why too often in federal countries the central state imposes its own will on the constituent member states by making use of its spending power, imposing its ideological outlook and by emulating a Jacobin tradition.

In this work, I contend that respecting the federal principle allows for the exercise of advanced democratic practices within nation-states by permitting internal nations to openly affirm the bases of their adherence to a common political project while also nourishing the development of the distinct collective traditions that benefit all parties to the association. Public debate in such sociological circumstances must be based on constant negotiations, supporting an ethos of deliberation within which justice-based arguments premised on the normative force of diversity will prevail. Only in such a scenario will an authentic and shared loyalty, as opposed to the instrumental sentiments of belonging engendered by procedural territorial federal models, underpin multination states and ensure their stability.

In recent years, many countries around the world have embraced the federal approach as the best means of dealing with the challenges of modernity. Experts consider federalism to be uniquely equipped to facilitate recognition of ethnic and cultural groups, promote representation of different currents of thought, guarantee the rights of national minorities, establish a fair division of power among orders of government, and establish an equitable distribution of wealth.

Contemporary states must address the challenge of national diversity because, on the one hand, most states are already experiencing it and, on the other hand, immigration is a feature of the modern world that is gradually becoming an unavoidable reality.[1] Federalism is thus a promising avenue for advanced liberal democracies and, as we will see in this book, multinational federalism is probably the optimal means of asserting collective identities and managing conflicts between communities. The political culture of such democracies is fertile ground for the values underlying the federal endeavour. Alfred Stepan rightly notes that "every single longstanding democracy in a territorially based multilingual and multinational polity is a federal state".[2] We need to explore the implications of this observation in greater detail with respect to advanced democracies.

While it may not be a panacea in itself and while, despite expectations, it has not always produced favourable outcomes, the federal formula has essential features that can increase the stability of political regimes. Significant democratic advances have been achieved when majority groups have agreed to treat other groups equitably in the name of community diversity. Naturally, tensions that cannot be ignored will arise when dealing with community relations. But the ability of all sides to freely return to the bargaining table and to arrive at compromises must be guaranteed if the federal vision is not to be diminished. The federal formula is thus a process in which there is deliberation and negotiation, and in which nations' futures are undetermined.

The present work could have focused on a wide range of cases because the federal approach has been advanced as a political solution in many contexts, including Indonesia, Iraq, Nigeria and Russia. In those countries, democracy has often been mismanaged and the federal spirit has not emerged. In this book, I will focus mainly on the case of Canada, but with a view to situations in other federal countries (e.g. Belgium and the United States) and in countries that are in the process of federalization (e.g. Spain and the United Kingdom). As we will see, establishing a federal system requires that the country be able to rely on advanced democratic practices, an expressed will to share territory, and respect for different traditions, all of which give meaning to the desire to live together. Meeting these requirements ensures the loyalty of all the partners in the federal whole and contributes to its sustainability.

Federalism and federation

First, we must make a distinction between the notions of federalism and federation.[3] Specialists of federalism have often employed the two concepts imprecisely. The former refers to traditions, a culture, a spirit, a way of acting and even an ideology. The latter concerns institutions.

It is possible to be in a situation in which a number of states have been incorporated into a federation but societal diversity has not been formally recognized in the functioning of its institutions. This is the situation in Germany, in Australia and in the United States. Rather surprisingly, it was an American, William Livingston,[4] who identified the recognition of societal diversity as a foundation of the federal spirit. Canada provides a different example because it is a federation, formed in 1867, that has sought over time to discard some of its federal features in pursuit of a more homogenizing vision. This trend has been the principal cause of major tensions between the English- and French-speaking communities in the country.[5] In Canada, two primary federal traditions co-exist: a tradition constructed around the notion of territorial federalism, which tends to obscure ethnic and cultural differences by advancing standardizing government policies, and a tradition based on the notion of multinationality that is espoused by the Québécois and First Nations. Canada is in the process of abandoning a set of conditions that are favourable to the recognition of differentiated self-governing entities, making it increasingly unlikely that Québec's specificity will be accommodated. This trend explains the frequent tensions between the promoters of the two federal traditions and the growth of the Québec nationalist movement.

Spain is not a federation in the strict sense. It has a unique institutional structure that can be termed a "state of autonomies".[6] Spain's social composition is very diverse. It comprises the three historical nations of Catalonia, Galicia and the Basque Country, as well as other communities that were quick to claim the status of the first three (Andalusia, Aragon, the Canary Islands and Valencia). This rich social diversity has led researchers to acknowledge, as William Livingston has done in regard to the United States, that federal features underlie the "state of autonomies". In this sense, Spain is inspired by federalism even though it is not a federation, properly speaking.

Like Spain, which was founded on ancient kingdoms, Belgium was initially formed out of small states that were integrated in a rather loose manner before being transformed into a unitary regime at the time of the French Conquest of 1794–1795.[7] Thus, the Jacobin model was imposed on Belgium. This imposition had profound repercussions for the way government business was managed and certainly contributed to the development of the distrust with which the Walloon and Flemish communities treated each other for most of the twentieth century. In response, a wide range of constitutional reforms have been promoted since the 1970s, all of which have been designed to make Belgium more federal.[8]

There is a wide range of federal experiments, and studying them can be enlightening. The examples of Belgium, Canada and Spain confirm that societal diversity is not always welcomed by those in power and that it is thus important that political communities participate in the expository work essential to having their legitimate claims acknowledged in federal political institutions.[9] Such expository work can be done in various ways and according to processes specific to different polities. For example, it can be done through commissions of inquiry, referenda, general elections, or constituent assemblies held to raise awareness in the various communities that are original parties to the federal pact.

Considering the recent referendum in which Catalonia was accorded a new political status in contemporary Spain, we need to understand the federal spirit that must accompany the creation of institutions that can take social diversity into account and provide sustainable means of accommodating communities.

Territorial and multinational federalism

As already mentioned, there are two types of federations, each of which has different political goals. On the one hand, there are "territorial" federations that propose treating all citizens in the same way. On the other hand, there is multinational federalism, which provides for equitable measures that ensure the same possibilities for achievement to the members of every national community in the federation. Territorial federations, such as the United States, Germany and Australia, have long been the favourites of specialists of federalism. However, government policies in territorial federations have largely ignored the needs of ethnic, cultural and national minorities (e.g. Blacks in the United States, Turks in Germany and Aboriginals in Australia). These minorities find themselves in countries that offer advancement to all through simple policies of positive discrimination which, it must be acknowledged, while they may have soothed the consciences of politicians, have had rather modest results in that they have not helped members of minority communities in significant measure.

The 1990s and 2000s opened the way to a new means of managing national diversity through greater acceptance of multinational federalism. The American model of territorial federalism, which had long been dominant, was challenged in countries characterized by significant national diversity, such as Belgium, Canada, Spain and the United Kingdom. While the latter two are not federations in the strict sense, their social foundations nonetheless make them complex states and, according to authors such as Livingston, will lead them towards federalism.

In recent years, all of these states have experienced major political changes. Belgium has undergone a number of constitutional reforms that have transformed it from a unitary state to a federation in less than a generation. Canada has missed significant opportunities by failing to satisfy Québec's proponents of multinational federalism, thereby leading to two referenda on Québec sovereignty. Spain has managed to turn its back on its totalitarian past by proposing a "state of autonomies", but still hesitates to accept asymmetrical systems that would meet the expectations of the various national communities on which its legitimacy is nevertheless based. Finally, the United Kingdom, a unitary state like Spain, has accepted the path of recognizing the country's original national communities, and is undertaking a major decentralization of powers.[10]

These changes have resulted in clashes between members of the majority community and members of national minorities. The success of the attempted reforms depends largely on the majority group's willingness to accept that political channels should remain open to negotiations and new demands from the various stakeholders. As James Tully notes:

> Freedom in a multinational society depends on members of that society being free to initiate discussions and negotiations on possible amendments to the existing framework of recognition, and a corollary is that other members have a *duty* to respond to legitimate demands. A member group that seeks recognition as a nation (in a form that is itself open to discussion) is free in so far as the possibility of discussion, negotiation and amendment is not in practice blocked by arbitrary constraints. If there is such an obstacle, the country's Constitution must be considered a straightjacket or structure of domination. In Canada, such absence of freedom can be illustrated by the cases of both Québec and the First Nations.[11]

The transition from territorial federalism to multinational federalism is a major qualitative step forward for minority nations in that it is the condition par excellence for freedom in existing countries.

The federal condition in Canada and Spain

The work of Donald Smiley, one of the leading specialists of Canadian federalism, has highlighted the advantages that federalism offers democratic societies while acknowledging that federalism is not a panacea for all problems pertaining to representation. In *The Federal Condition in Canada*, Smiley explores the federal features that are essential for smooth government in Canada. His analysis highlights a number of important aspects of the Canadian federation, including the duality at the foundation of the federating pact, the relations between the centre and the periphery with respect to territorial economic conflicts, and the relative autonomy of the central government and the federation's member states in terms of their ability to influence the course of history.[12] Throughout the present discussion, we will also see why a complex liberal society is the form of organization most conducive to federalism. The central argument is related to the fact that federalism challenges the monist conception[13] that has tended to dominate since the beginnings of modernity.

Thus, in order to understand federalism and its contribution to dispute management, we first have to establish four key points. First, the principle of federalism requires that there be no overlap of powers so that levels of government may have great freedom in their exercise of shared sovereignty. Second, respect for the autonomy of political entities must be enforced in the advancement of joint initiatives, thereby encouraging the establishment of structures for exchange and collaboration. Third, when these conditions are met, trust between political players is maintained more easily, and even consolidated, and initiatives for bringing the communities together become possible. Finally, making these principles concrete is conducive to the development of loyalty to the federation, which is also one of the pillars of collaboration among the various communities because it ensures solidarity between all strata of society and all orders of government.

Pierre Elliott Trudeau, Prime Minister of Canada from 1968 to 1979 and from 1980 to 1984, noted that "democracy is a value in itself, which cannot be sacrificed to considerations of expediency, likewise at certain times and in certain places federalism may be held to be a fundamental value…"[14] This has been true in various cases; for example, in Spain.

Without reviewing the history of Spain here, let us note some of the key periods that contributed to developing the idea of federalism on the Iberian peninsula. There have been a number of movements in support of federalism since the mid-nineteenth century. The first dates back to the 1840s, when Spain began a process of liberal political reform. It was also at that time that Republicans and Democrats formed a coalition in support of federalism. Inspired by thinkers such as Proudhon, Tocqueville and Krausista, federal thought in Spain at the time focused on two main issues: recognition of Spain's heterogeneity and decentralization of power.[15]

Throughout the nineteenth century, federalism was a basis for opposition to the centralizing policies underlying Spanish political liberalism. Aside from Carlism,[16] federalism thus became the only serious alternative to these centralizing ideas. The kind of federalism in question differed from Carlism in that it was anchored in towns and was socially progressive. The next wave of federal thought was characterized by the work of Pi i Margall, who was from Catalonia. His work, which contains in-depth discussions of the American, Swiss and German constitutions and which was strongly influenced by Proudhon, helped spread federal ideas. For example, in his masterwork, *Las Nacionalidades*, published in 1877, Pi i Margall sets out three key ideas:

1 The principle of autonomy for affairs internal to the state and the principle of heteronomy for external affairs.
2 The inalienable sovereignty of individuals.
3 The replacement of the notion of power with that of consent.[17]

Pi i Margall was already thinking of the central role of the pact among constituents. He also promoted the principle of unity in diversity, which was to become common ground for federalists. As Isidre Molas[18] notes, Margall insisted that Spain's unity depended largely on its economic unity, while at the same time admitting that Spain was a shared homeland. He also advocated abandoning the principle of unity in Spain because, according to him, and this is what is interesting, it was precisely this principle that endangered the unity of the country. According to Pi i Margall, Spain's unity depended on the acceptance, respect and promotion of the fundamental differences that characterized it. His ideas were extremely revolutionary for his time, and remain so today.

While they lost some of their vitality over time, federalist and autonomist ideas began to regain strength in the 1930s, and the notion of integral federalism became more salient in Spain.[19] The integral federalism of the first half of the 1930s, which was known much more for its decentralizing thrust than for its openness to regional specificities, was not very popular in Catalonia, Galicia and the Basque Country, where it was not seen as particularly advantageous. The idea underlying integral federalism is to absorb historical nations in a democratic manner and to abandon regional rights in order to establish a modern, progressive, integrating Spain open to all forms of diversity (including regional particularities). The new integral Spain would be a meeting place for pluralist nationalists from the periphery and unitary Spanish republicans.

The state of autonomies in 1978 presented political players with the same challenges: how could they convince people to live together when some sought to establish a universalizing citizenship that would give everyone the same rights (even when fair, equitable access to such rights varied considerably depending on whether or not one belonged to the nation known as "Spanish") and others wished to belong to the country through another primary identity at the level of an historical area?

This is still the challenge facing the state of autonomies because the rise of minority nationalism in Spain, Canada, the United Kingdom and elsewhere reveals an inability to secure the endorsement of all citizens for a common project that could accommodate diversity in federal and federalizing states. Shedding light on this reality is the central goal of this book.

Overview of the chapters

This book is structured along three main lines: the foundations, normative arguments and values on which the federal project is based; changes in federalism in multinational contexts; and the emergence of the multination as an optimal solution for countries characterized by national diversity.

In Chapter 1, we review the role of memory in the construction of modern nations by briefly exploring the Catalan and Québécois identities. Naturally, Catalonia and Québec grew out of different political contexts, but historically both were exposed to federal ideas and have often promoted such ideas. The discussion will provide material essential for our analysis by showing the context in which these two nations are developing.

In Chapter 2, we discuss federalism in terms of normative values and show that asymmetrical federalism makes it possible to strengthen democracy by redistributing powers, encouraging citizen participation, increasing the legitimacy of the political system and helping to accommodate minority nations within institutions. Establishing federalism thus improves procedural liberalism by valuing the contributions of communities rather than focusing solely on individual citizens.

In Chapter 3, after having noted the rise of the multination in a number of advanced liberal democracies, we explain how ideas have developed along two contradictory lines. The primary trend in the countries in question has been to advance public policy without regard for social diversity, but with a view to ensuring uniform treatment for every individual. Such equal treatment masks grave injustice because the members of different national communities do not have the same access to power or chances for advancement in society. In order to gain a better understanding of the issues in question, we propose an analysis of Pierre Elliott Trudeau's proceduralist political project and also of the philosophical communitarian counterpart advanced by Charles Taylor. Confronted with the emerging multination phenomenon in a number of contemporary states, Taylor's argument is seen as the more appropriate approach to dealing with national minorities living in advanced liberal democracies.

In Chapter 4, we propose a means of revitalizing executive federalism in order to enable representatives of different national communities to establish fair and equitable relationships with central government bodies. We analyse the evolution of Canadian federalism from its founding in 1867 to the present, and draw lessons from the various episodes that have provoked major tensions between Québec and the rest of Canada over the last 30 years. If multinational federalism that would meet the expectations of the Québécois and attenuate the constitutional crisis cannot be achieved in the short term in Canada, we suggest that bilateral relations between Québec and the central government should be encouraged through executive federalism. We believe this would open the channels of communication between the two main political communities in Canada.

In Chapter 5, we demonstrate how the rise of Canadian nationalism has directly weakened federal ideas in Canada and contributed to the unprecedented mobilization of the Québécois nation around Québec as a state. In order to describe this dynamic more fully, three areas of public policy are examined in greater detail: the Canadian Social Union, international relations, and the imposition of the Canadian Charter of Rights and Freedoms in 1982.

In Chapter 6, we focus on theory in order to develop a more complete understanding of the heritage that influences the way that political actors think about power relations and that often prevents them from looking beyond high-profile short-term strategies. We look at three bodies of work that have influenced the way that community conflicts are managed, namely, the works of John Rawls, Daniel Elazar and Ernest Renan. The ideas of these three thinkers are described in turn, and lessons are drawn for the cases of Canada and European countries, in particular Spain. Establishing multinational federalism in these countries is proposed as a promising means for reconciling national communities within larger wholes.

In conclusion, we establish the urgent need to use the multination as a basis for action and thought so that contemporary actors will have the right tools to meet the greatest challenge of our time: recognizing national minority communities within large political bodies. In short, countries today must recognize the diversity that defines them, and develop new institutions that will allow national communities to fully achieve their democratically advanced collective goals. This result would legitimize action and bring communities together.

1 Memory and national identity in Catalonia and Québec[1]

> For each individual to discover in himself what his humanity consists in, he needs a horizon of meaning, which can only be provided by some allegiance, group membership, cultural tradition. He needs, in the broadest sense, a language in which to ask and answer the questions of ultimate significance.[2]

The above epigraph by Charles Taylor identifies language, culture and a feeling of belonging as crucial for the construction of one's identity. Taylor made the remark in the spring of 1979, one year before Québec's first referendum on sovereignty-association in which the forces of Québec sovereignty saw their political project rejected by three out of five voters. That referendum should have led to major constitutional reforms so that the Québécois would feel more comfortable in the Canadian federation. However, while there were reforms, they were largely aimed at consolidating power in the hands of the central government. This only strengthened the sovereignty movement in Québec by giving it a major reason to mobilize.

Throughout his career, Taylor has defended general liberal values, and many of his writings have denounced the risks that individualism poses to political communities, though he has been careful not to suggest independence for nations such as Québec that have questioned their membership in composite states. Indeed, Taylor hesitates to assert that all options be open to nations at the foundations of existing states because

> it becomes very important that we be recognized for what we are. If this is denied or set at naught by those who surround us, it is extremely difficult to maintain a horizon of meaning by which to identify ourselves.[3]

Taylor's words take on their full meaning when they are applied to Catalonia and Québec, the cases to which I will essentially limit the discussion in this chapter because their liberal approaches are informative for all multinational societies. Indeed, Taylor's words echo demands for recognition that have been reiterated frequently throughout history by political spokespersons in Catalonia and Québec. For Taylor, the central problem of misrecognition leads minority nations to seek a status that corresponds more closely to the perception they have of themselves.[4] Here is how Taylor summarizes his position:

> The thesis is that our identity is partly shaped by recognition or its absence, often by the *mis*recognition of others, and so a person or group of people can suffer real damage, real distortion, if the people or society around them mirror back to them a confining or demeaning or contemptible picture of themselves. Nonrecognition or misrecognition can inflict harm, can be a form of oppression, imprisoning someone in a false, distorted, and reduced mode of being.[5]

Catalonia and Québec are surprising both because of their resilience over the centuries and because of their ability to advance their respective nationalist projects. With a view to the recent positive results in the 18 June 2006 referendum on a new political status for Catalonia within Spain, and the negative result of the Québec referendum on 30 October 1995, we have to identify and understand nations' needs to be recognized on their own terms and to portray themselves to others according to their own dynamics. We also need to acknowledge the sometimes freewheeling backroom intrigues and manoeuvring of the various political and social players involved in constructing and affirming national identity. Current challenges, including that of acquiring formal recognition as nations within the Spanish and Canadian constitutions, require great solidarity on the part of Catalonian and Québec leaders, and long-lasting, solid commitment from civil society.

Québec is an extremely relevant case for Catalonia since it has already held two referenda on its political status in the Canadian federation and is still seeking full recognition as a nation. Throughout its history, Québec has also engaged in major political struggles against the establishment of majority pan-Canadian nationalism, and has sought, like the people of Catalonia, to highlight its specificity as a historical nation in a federation.

The challenges that these two nations face largely explain why Catalonian and Québec political theorists are often invited to

Wallonia, Wales and Scotland to participate in discussions on the importance of establishing fair relations between the central government and member states of complex countries (such as Belgium, Italy and the United Kingdom). Such theorists generally argue in favour of liberal projects based on territorial recognition in order to give national communities greater empowerment and social cohesion, while at the same time insisting that the political representatives of national communities be directly accountable to their constituents. Such prescriptions often differ from the policies in fashion in Canada and Spain; for example, those based on the principle of non-territoriality, generally expressed as *café para todos* in Spain and "a province is a province is a province" in Canada, that are designed to prevent identity claims from gaining a foothold, no matter how legitimate the claims might be. Thus, among Catalans and Québécois, claims are presented more in terms of fair treatment, whereas members of majority nations speak of equal treatment. Obviously, requiring that all citizens or all member states of federations be subject to identical treatment favours the majority national group.

The present chapter will be organized along four main lines. First, I will explore the theme of memory and nation-building to explain political differences between majority and minority nations. Then I will sketch the broad strokes of the defining events that have marked Catalonia and Québec by reviewing the way that liberal nationalism developed in those two historical nations.[6] We will then look at the affirmation of minority national cultures in the countries that currently seem most reluctant to meet demands for recognition. Finally, I will focus on the Catalan, Scottish and Québec cases to provide a short analysis of the plural identities that citizens claim in multinational situations.

Memory and national construction

A sociological and political approach anchored in history is essential for describing the birth and development of nations such as Acadia, Catalonia, Galicia and Québec. First, I would like to cite Fernand Dumont, a pioneer of sociology in Québec, who, like Salvador Giner with respect to Catalonia,[7] has described the shape and depths of the soul of Québec.

> Survival is impossible if the past is not invoked since a nation that is first and foremost a culture comes down to a heritage. The dual recourse to hope and memory is justification. It is also a

guarantee of permanence, for the result is, through the power of
the written word, the edification of a *reference* that will portray a
present people in history.[8]

In these few sentences, Dumont has summarized the stakes for minority national communities as they seek to assert themselves. Writing
the history of a nation or political community is a political action par
excellence; it is also a means of raising awareness and projecting the
group into the future. According to Dumont, it is imperative to look
to the past in order to understand the present. Indeed, this was also
recognized by members of the Catalan Renaissance movement
(*Renaixança*), who were swept up by a wave of romanticism in the
mid-nineteenth century. The members of the movement helped establish the Catalan language, gave historical meaning to the nation and
spread Catalan culture.[9] However, to return to Taylor, "Nations exist
not just where there is the objective fact of speaking the same language and sharing a common history, but where this is subjectively
reflected in a people's identifications."[10]

Writing not only expresses a culture undergoing change, but also
the continuity of daily creation. Benedict Anderson describes this as
the incarnation of the imagined community.[11] Literature becomes
simultaneously an exercise in identity creation, a way of thinking, a
point of view, a manner of seeing oneself and a means of projecting
oneself into the future.

Thus, understanding the phenomenon of nationality requires
better knowledge and recognition of institutions, which is why the
educational system, religion, family, unions, political parties and
social movements are so important. Such networks hold great potential. The processes of socialization are very important in the construction of a society because they give meaning to history and serve as
reference points[12] and stabilizing features.

It is less important to idealize the past than it is to attempt to
understand it, including the successes and the failures, as objectively
as possible in its historical framework. Québec and Catalonia will be
better equipped to face their respective futures and project themselves
into history as it is being written if they have fully accepted their
pasts. Accepting the past includes agreeing to situate oneself in relation to others. This creates awareness of the distinctive features of the
political community and truly establishes the democratic structure of
liberalism. Too often in procedural liberalism, national pluralism is
ignored even though it reflects the feeling of belonging and, by extension, the expression of the general will.[13]

In his ground-breaking work, *Genèse de la société québécoise*, Fernand Dumont makes another important observation, which is also very relevant for Catalonia: he notes that Québec society "is mainly structured at its base".[14] Dumont rightly points out that Québec society is rooted in a wide set of networks of social exchanges in which shared experiences are anchored in a specific context. This thesis has been taken up and expanded by a new generation of researchers, such as Luc Turgeon in his work on the central role of civil society at the time of the Quiet Revolution in Québec.[15]

Catalonia and Québec are developing differently from other member states of Spain and Canada. Although it seems like only yesterday, 60 years have in fact passed since Pierre Vilar noted that in the case of Catalonia there were "growing dissimilarities between the social structure of the Catalan area and that of the majority of the rest of the country [Spain]".[16] In Spain, civil society has played a truly central role in maintaining social cohesion, a trend that continues to this day. The same dissonance characterizes the relations between Québec and the rest of Canada, where two host societies have had to integrate various waves of immigrants since the end of the Second World War. In fact, there are two citizenship regimes into which people are invited as full participants.[17]

In a way, Catalonia and Québec are region-states[18] or, to borrow Simon Langlois' accurate description, "global societies"[19] with well-defined social structures, historically anchored distinct cultures, specific political institutions and clearly identifiable territory. This makes these two nations unique host societies[20] in Canada and Spain.

Defining events: Catalonia's journey

In the history of a people, certain points can be seen as interpretive keys that make it easier to understand the economic, social and political changes that the people has undergone.

First, note that the Catalan *comarques* (i.e. principalities ruled by Counts) date back to the ninth century and continued to play a major role until the Bourbon dynasty in 1715.[21] These principalities presided over the region's commercial and political destiny from the twelfth to the fifteenth centuries. "[T]he principalities of Catalan had a form of constitution limiting the 'sovereign's' powers before the famous English Magna Carta came into existence."[22] The principalities had a much greater impact on the construction of contemporary Catalan identity than we tend to suspect.

Under the Bourbon regime, the *Nueva Planta* decree pertaining to Catalonia was passed in 1715 and led to Castilanization of the public service under the Crown of Aragon, which controlled the Kingdom. In response, Catalans fell back on civil society. Until then, Catalonia had never had a strong government because during the Habsburg reign in Spain, non-Castilian areas were essentially autonomous territories. The arrival of the Bourbons led to the disappearance of Catalan institutions and the elimination of the medieval structures favouring Catalan regional nobility.

Subsequently, social mobility in Catalonia was tied to the emergence of a truly Catalonian industrial bourgeoisie, such as in the textile industry. However, the Bourbons were partly responsible for Catalan economic achievements because they provided access to both the Castilian market and their vast empire.[23] This helped to consolidate Catalonia's economy and facilitated the establishment of an elite class of merchants.

At the time, Catalans had little access to positions in the public service and in the army. For example, towards the end of the eighteenth century, "half of the public servants of Aragon were Castilians, [rising to] 60% in Catalonia..".[24] Note also that in Spanish governments "between 1833 and 1902, out of 900 ministers, only 25 were from Catalonia (2.7% though the area contained over 10% of Spain's population). [...] between that date [1902] and 1914, no Catalan was appointed minister".[25]

During that time, neither the public service nor the army were avenues that Catalans could use to advance in society. Catalans' exclusion from central government institutions led them to invest more in Catalan counties and provinces. The provinces were created when the Constitution was adopted at Cadix in 1812, and put an end to the principalities. The authors of the Constitution had a simple idea: "to reduce differentiating features, to harmonize, to standardize."[26] In other words, they hoped to reduce to a minimum the diversity on which the existing regime was founded so as to produce as much cohesion as possible and prevent the emergence of sources of opposition.

The number of provinces varied from one period to the next, but they were frequently used for the same purpose, namely to prevent communities from mobilizing within the former principalities. Thus, the principality of Catalonia was initially divided into four provinces: Barcelona, Girona, Lleida and Tarragona. It is plausible to suggest that the provinces were created and employed for purely centralizing purposes because they made their representatives essential and unavoidable conduits to the central government. The desire to centralize was later expressed in various ways, such as in the attempt to create a centralized bureau of statistics, the imposition in 1868 of the peseta as the monetary unit, and the 1889 establishment of the first Spanish Civil Code.

The political project of a federal constitution for all of Spain at the time of the First Republic cannot be ignored. It had a profound impact on Catalonia's structure since Catalans saw it as creating a possibility for advancing the federal spirit. There was talk of a new state composed of historically constituted regions and of various forms of autonomy for individuals, municipalities, regions and nations, all of which are components of Spain. Establishment of the First Republic helped to structure a truly Catalan identity in that it gave Catalan people a greater sense of history. According to historians such as Albert Balcells, the failure of the First Republic was a defining event for Catalonia's political orientation, and led to stronger assertion of Catalan nationalism.[27]

In 1888, Catalan representatives asked the King to establish an independent legislative assembly to debate issues concerning the region and to recognize Catalan as an official language. Following this, a number of pressure groups, including the Catalan Union in 1892, and political parties, such as the *Lliga Regionalista* in 1901 and the *Solidaritat Catalana* coalition in 1907,[28] emerged and used nationalism as a spearhead. *Solidaritat Catalana* won seats in all four Catalan provinces in the election. A few years later, in 1913, the four provinces merged to form the *Mancommunitat de Catalunya*.[29] That experiment ended in April 1925 in the wake of the 1923 coup d'état led by Miguel Primo de Rivera, but it contributed both to bringing the community of Catalan provinces closer together through common policies in education, economics and language learning, and to increasing solidarity among Republican forces throughout Spain. This led to the Second Spanish Republic (1931–1936), in which Catalans played a more significant political role. At the same time, Catalonia regained autonomy by establishing the *Generalitat* (1931–1938), though it was short-lived because General Franco decreed an end to it in April 1938 in the midst of the Spanish Civil War (1936–1939). Civil liberties were then suspended, and the legislation ratified by the *Generalitat* abolished. Public and official use of the Catalan language was prohibited by decree as of 16 February 1939. These political actions had major repercussions for the construction of the Catalan identity, which was forced to assert itself in the resistance.

This was the *Estado nuevo* period in which all forms of opposition were forbidden. Catalonia was thus reduced to a simple territory of Spain. A second *renaixença* began in the late 1950s when intellectuals and artists gradually revived the Catalan movement, that included Maria del Mar, Pi de la Serra and LLuis Llach. Resistance became more organized and powerful.

Still, today in Catalonia, the notion of centralism remains associated with dictatorship and with the imposition of majority nationalism, while autonomy corresponds to a time of individual and community freedoms. It is important to note that when the new democratic age began in Spain, King Juan Carlos chose to give his first official speech as head of state in Catalonia,[30] and made another major political statement by delivering part of it in Catalan.

King Juan Carlos' action was crucial for two main reasons: it marked the beginning of the reconciliation of the two nations within a plural Spain, and it increased recognition of a culture and nation that were completely rooted in history. It also established the "state of autonomies" that confirmed Spain's multinational nature. The *Generalitat* was restored in September 1977 in exchange for President Josep Tarradellas' recognition of the monarchy of Juan Carlos. This asserted an important principle of constitutionalism: mutual recognition, the key to bringing communities together.

The political powers of Spain's Right and Left then began seeking means of reducing the significance of historical communities as a basis for the new Spain. They tried to persuade other autonomous communities to employ Article 137 of the 1978 Constitution[31] as quickly as possible. The purpose was clear: to make all autonomous communities interchangeable players on the political level and to erase all distinctions between those communities. As Miguel Herrero de Minon might have said, it was a way of limiting the contribution of the "differential societies"[32] that Spain had chosen as a means of returning to the democratic path after Franco's death.

It is nonetheless surprising to see that, after all of the excesses that historical nations have suffered in Spain, particularly during the twentieth century, it is "finally the Spanish nation that is retained as the sole repository of sovereignty, and therefore the foundation of the new constitutional order".[33] However, Spain now has to take into account the legitimate and essential contributions of historical nations in the constitutional process.[34] Catalonia's new status was accepted by Catalans on 18 June 2006, and takes the logic of recognition a little further, even though the advance is seen as insufficient by a large portion of the region's population. The primary challenge facing a state such as Spain is that of succeeding in instituting a new constitutional regime that obtains Catalans' allegiance to a country that has often imposed coercive political control throughout history and that now sometimes gives the impression of wanting to use national diversity as a means of bringing people together.

Defining events: Québec's journey

What are the principal interpretive keys to understanding contemporary Québec? As in the case of Catalonia, we cannot overlook the past, rivalries between various players, and the various traditions that have been prominent in political struggles.

The first defining moment of Québécois identity was, according to one reading, the Conquest of 1759, and, according to another reading, France's transfer of its land in North America to England in 1763 under the Treaty of Paris. Even though there is no clear consensus on how to interpret these events, there is clear suggestion that the *first Canadiens* (who came to identify themselves as Québécois in the 1960s) experienced a bitter defeat or of an equally disappointing abandonment that further impoverished Québécois' image of their past. Thus, there is no myth about an autonomous kingdom, as there was in the case of Catalonia, but instead a story of humiliating defeat and abandonment by the country of origin.

Beaten in the Conquest, the *Canadiens* subsequently came under the authority of the British Crown. Naturally, that had major consequences on *Canadiens*' feelings towards their former homeland, France, which had abandoned them to keep colonies it considered more profitable in the West Indies, and towards their conqueror, the British Empire, which had defeated them and made Québec an English colony. *Canadiens* were required to renounce Catholicism and abide by common law, although in practice they continued to obey French civil law.[35] The bijural system was de facto established at that time.[36]

The second key point in the construction of Québec nationality was the passage of the Québec Act in June 1774 at a time when the American colonies were rebelling against England in an attempt to separate from the Empire. English authorities required French Canadians to pledge allegiance to the British Crown from then on. In theory, this pledge of allegiance gave them access to public and political positions, though in reality those French Canadians who attained such positions were the exceptions. When the Québec Act was ratified, freedom of religion was re-established, use of the French language was accepted and the seigneurial system was maintained.[37] At that time the co-existence of French civil law and British criminal law was made official. This gave Québec a foundation upon which to define itself as, to use the expression employed in Canada, a distinct society, or if one prefers, as a "differential society".

Thus, the Québec Act confirmed the distinct nature of Québec in the vast British Empire. Indeed, remarkably, it was the first time that the British Empire had agreed to ratify a constitution that gave legitimate foundations to one of its colonies.[38] Rights were not extinguished but affirmed. Future generations later revived the claims in the face of historical and political conditions that were most often unfavourable to the Québécois, who found themselves a shrinking minority in Canada.

There is no consensus on the Act among social scientists in Canada. Some have vilified it as an abuse of imperial power and seen it as a simple tactic designed to deal with the thirteen rebellious American colonies.[39] Others have seen it as something with potential for Québec that has not been sufficiently tapped. For example, see James Tully's work on how the Royal Proclamation contributed to recognition of Aboriginal claims and on the Québec Act's contribution to the assertion of Québec nationalism and the legitimization of the Québécois' claims as one of Canada's founding peoples.[40]

While insufficient in many respects, the Québec Act is an essential point of departure that has made it possible for today's Québécois to identify the institutional source of their national claims, and especially to establish the legitimacy of those claims. In other words, it is in fact a key document that is prior to the Constitution Act 1867 but contains principles that must be respected by political players unless, of course, Québec decides to reject them.

In other words, the Québec Act plays the same role as the Royal Proclamation of 1763 does for the First Nations in that it provides a primary legal foundation for Québec's historical claims. By legitimizing ancient customs, traditions and a specific legal regime, the Québec Act is an exceptional reference point for the Québécois, though it is still criticized by some.[41] Moreover, it thus affirms the general principles of constitutionalism that are at the heart of constitutional negotiations in Canada and that were renewed in the British North America Act (to which Québec assented) that was signed in 1867 and in the Constitution Act 1982, even though this act was ratified against the will of Québec's National Assembly.

Gérard Bouchard acknowledges the Québec Act's importance when he writes, "By recognizing the rights and specificities of French-speaking Canadians, in a way, the 1774 Act promoted the awakening of national awareness."[42] Bouchard could not have been more perceptive. A few years later, the Constitutional Act of 1791 was adopted. It consisted in rethinking Canada along the lines of an ethnic cleavage that divided English and French Canadians such that each constituted a majority on their own land.

The 1837–1838 rebellions are another key point in Québec's emergence as a nation in the period dominated by British rule. The rebellions broke out simultaneously in Lower and Upper Canada, and focused on the defence of Republican and certain liberal values. London did not take kindly to the uprisings, and in 1840 passed the Union Act, the primary purpose of which was to merge Lower and Upper Canada and thus make English-speakers the majority in Canada.

The third key point in the construction of Québec nationalism was the 1867 Confederation pact. The pact between two founding peoples confirmed the founding fathers' wish to advance identity-based pluralism by recognizing, albeit implicitly as Guy Laforest has pointed out,[43] the presence of English and French Canadians at the heart of emerging political institutions. Contemporary history reminds us that there were major misunderstandings[44] of the policies on both sides of the linguistic divide because expectations appear to have differed.[45]

The Government of Québec has frequently relied on the interpretation based on the presence of two founding peoples in its presentations to the central government. At the time of the Rowell–Sirois Commission (1937–1940) hearings on the division of powers between the members of the federation and the central government, the representatives of the Québec government noted that the initial 1867 constitution was a pact, and used the opportunity to again point out that

> in 1867, a certain number of states, known as provinces, autonomous and sovereign under the British Crown, having decided to come together, agreed to form a federation and deliberately rejected the legislative union system because that system, with the centralization of power that it entails, provides no guarantees for minorities. In order to establish the federation, the provinces agreed to transfer to the federal body a certain portion of their powers, but they kept, in addition to the legislative powers that were not transferred, the political entity. They have thus remained, in their own spheres, sovereign states ... the Confederation is a

pact voluntarily agreed to and it cannot be amended except with the consent of all.[46]

This pronouncement by representatives of the Government of Québec reminded the Commissioners, who were mandated to make recommendations on the functioning of the Canadian federation, that the central government cannot ignore the founding principles at the core of the constitutional pact. There are three general principles: continuity, mutual recognition and consent.[47] While they were sometimes mishandled by the central government between 1867 and 1982, when the first Canadian constitutional regime ended, those principles are at the heart of the federal spirit and constitute the essential foundations upon which the legitimacy of the Canadian state is based.

The establishment of a new constitutional regime in 1982, with the patriation of the Constitution from Great Britain and the entrenchment of the Canadian Charter of Rights and Freedoms (see Chapter 5), was a major attack on the three principles at the base of constitutionalism in Canada. It created a shock wave that affected the whole political class and led to a huge popular movement in Québec in the decades that followed. It also gave rise to many

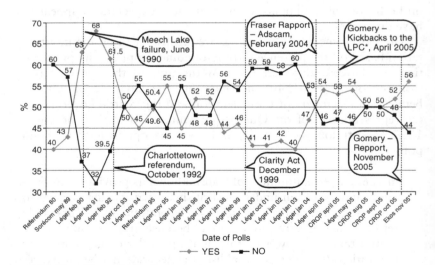

*LPC: Liberal Party of Canada
**All non respondents for the Ekos November 2005 poll given to the NO

Figure 1.1 Evolution of voting intentions for sovereignty in Québec, 1980–2005 (sovereignty-association or sovereignty-partnership).

initiatives, including the Bloc Québécois (a political party dedicated to the independence of Québec), which arrived in Ottawa in 1990, a second referendum in fifteen years on the issue of sovereignty and a movement in favour of specifically Québec citizenship.[48] Throughout the period, polls confirmed that popular support for the sovereignty of Québec often exceeded an absolute majority (see Figure 1.1).

Disregarding historical compromises and the three general principles underlying constitutionalism (continuity, mutual recognition and consent), the central government and nine English-speaking provinces put an end to the first Canadian constitutional regime (1867–1982) despite opposition that was expressed unanimously by all of the political parties represented in Québec's National Assembly.

It is ironic that the Canadian constitutional reform that began in the early 1960s specifically to meet Québec's needs was completed to the detriment of the Québec nation and without taking into account the demands for recognition expressed by its leaders. The imposition of a new constitutional regime in 1982 broke with historical continuity and cast aside the dualist vision which, up until this point, had been a defining feature of the Canadian federation.[49]

Affirmation of national cultures

It should be noted that the Catalan and Québec nations existed prior to Spain and Canada. Yet, Spain and Canada have always had difficulty recognizing and supporting the full expression of these nations' political and constitutional identities. In Canada, this was seen in the discussions around the Meech Lake Accord that took place between 1987 and 1990, and around the Charlottetown Accord in 1992.[50] In Spain it was seen in 2005–2006 in the debate over recognition of the Catalan nation by the Spanish government.

As we saw at the beginning of the chapter, Spain as we know it today is the result of an aggregative process rather than a merger of a number of Christian principalities in the Middle Ages. The links to the principalities enabled each nation to maintain its institutions and continue to develop its own records of court decisions through the sixteenth and seventeenth centuries. After the War of the Spanish Succession, which ended in 1714, and Philip V's decrees, the Bourbons abolished the governments of the former principalities of Aragon, Catalonia, Valencia and the Balearic Islands, and also eliminated certain features of civil law and some special tax provisions. Until the nineteenth century, Navarre and the Basque Country kept their administrative and tax responsibilities, known as *los fueros*.

In the twentieth century, despite its opposite objective, the repression that the Catalans suffered under General Franco actually strengthened the Catalan identity. At that time, there was a coalition between the moderate right, centre and left. All ideologies (except the extreme right) rallied to the cause of national affirmation. However, Albert Balcells says in *El nacionalismo catalan* that the radical party of Alejandro Lerroux, whose influence was very strong among workers in the Barcelona area, was generally hostile to Catalan demands,[51] while the anarchist–unionist movement that arose from the *Confederacion Nacional del Trabajo* (CNT) remained rather indifferent.[52]

In recent years, the Spain of the ancient principalities and regions has reappeared, and Spanish nationalism has been denounced by many. Thus, today, democracy in Spain is channelled through establishment of the "state of autonomies". Paradoxically, despite the many excesses of Spanish nationalism, the Spanish nation was none-theless invested in 1978 as the sole repository of sovereignty in Spain. The new Spanish nation is now composed of a number of different nationalities, in other words, a set of nations within a state on the way to federalization.[53]

In Québec's case, the primary political players would like to put an end to all structures of domination by re-establishing the fundamental principles of constitutionalism. History, memory and identity must be employed by the political class to ensure that institutions adequately reflect the foundations on which the country was built and from which it draws its political legitimacy.

In a text that will probably stand the test of time, James Tully establishes that Québec is not currently free within the Canadian federation for at least three reasons. First, constitutional changes can be made to the way the federation operates without Québec's consent. Second, while Québec defines itself as a nation, it seems impossible to gain concrete recognition of this reality because doing so would require the consent of the other members of the federation and the central institutions. In other words, though it is a founding nation, Québec cannot make constitutional changes. Third, the present amending formula denies Québec's right to self-determination.

Yet, multinational societies, such as those of Canada and Spain, will be truly democratic only "in so far as the constitutional rules providing the framework of the association between the various nations are open to challenge and amendment".[54] The state's legitimacy is at stake. The objectives are less about affirmation and recognition of identity than they are about the establishment of "constitutional rules of mutual recognition" for the founding nations that are respected by all.[55] The quest for mutual recognition, historical continuity and consent remains at the heart of political debate. In short, it is impossible to sidestep this discussion, no matter what representatives of majority nations might think.

The political struggles and constitutional debates in recent years in Canada and Spain have articulated very authentic expressions of concerns. Tully's argument is directly related to the situation in Québec and Canada when he says that "the possibility for a nation to represent itself in different ways is one of the primary ferments of legitimacy and stability of contemporary political regimes. [...] Struggles for recognition are also means of discovering oneself."[56] Both the 1998 Declaration of Barcelona, in which the Catalan, Galician and Basque nationalist parties demand formal recognition of their nations within Spain, and the consensus reached on 30 September 2005 among the primary Catalan political parties concerning official recognition of the Catalan nation are perfect examples of the actualization of these nations. Likewise, in Canada, the 1980 and 1995 Québec referenda were high points in healthy deliberative democracy.

These debates encourage us to go beyond what Neil MacCormick calls "the ideological unity of the sovereign state".[57] It is in the degree to which the non-neutrality of the Canadian and Spanish states can become evident and that other legitimate expressions can be recognized that it will become possible to imagine other avenues of democratic accommodation and other ways of reconciling the past and present without ignoring history. As Dimitrios Karmis very perceptively points out in *Québec: État et société*, "to defend a conception of national identity that is supposed to be culturally neutral is to defend a monist conception of national identity that favours the majority cultural and linguistic group."[58] Thus, it is important in both the Canadian and Spanish cases that there be recognition of the presence and legitimacy of a *demos* that should be made concrete in plural form.

The constellation of belongings[59]

The demands of national minorities for recognition flow from the affirmation of their identities through history, their updating in the present and their projection into the future. It is most often through the expression of national identities that political actors manage to gain acknowledgement of visions of society that are specific to their nation. People living in culturally identified areas embedded in multinational states usually have a dual national identity, which suggests some hierarchization of belonging. This is what Charles Taylor is talking about when he refers, on the one hand, to a first-level identity that enables all citizens to recognize one another on a common, shared basis in an overall state and, on the other hand, to a second-level identity that enables people to be part of an analogous undertaking through national identity. Thus, Scots identify themselves first as members of the Scottish national community, just as do the Catalans and Québécois in their own cases, but they also belong to the United Kingdom, Spain and Canada respectively.

Naturally, this raises the question of national minorities' loyalty to the country. Note that Taylor insists that internal nations be allowed to exist fully and that institutions be designed to ensure their sustainability, otherwise they will feel alienated and seek other means of national affirmation. Taylor finds the federal formula adequate as a means of meeting the requirements of national pluralism so long as it is based on respect for national communities. According to Taylor, it is an optimal means of managing conflict between communities.

Sensitive to the national pluralism issue, Manuel Castells provides more food for thought by looking at the situation in the former Soviet Union, where political leaders tried to impose a single national identity using repressive ideological and military means.[60] The undertaking failed largely because the national construction that was imposed did not match the historical and sociological processes through which the country had been built.

In modern democratic countries, when members of a national minority have a dominant national identity, the national minority can provide an additional legitimate *context of choice*, to use Will Kymlicka's notion, and deliberately signal its presence to members of the majority community, thereby requiring those members to take the national minority fairly and equitably into account when designing public policy. The political expression of the demands of national minorities establishes power relations between the minorities and the majority, thereby contributing to "the creation of inter-subjective spaces in which people can exchange ideas about their identity-based differences and similarities".[61]

How does this apply to the Catalan, Scottish and Québec cases? How are the inter-subjective spaces of which Jocelyn Maclure speaks deployed? The most recent comparative data we have are for 1998 and 2005. It seems that Catalans' sense of identity has remained relatively stable, though there has been a small increase (from 11.5 per cent to 14.5 per cent) in the number of people surveyed who identify solely as Catalan, while the percentage of those who define themselves solely as Spanish has dropped (from 13.0 per cent to 7.7 per cent). Most of the people surveyed had a dual identity: in 2005, 23.4 per cent said they were more Catalan than Spanish, and 44.8 per cent declared they were just as Catalan as they were Spanish (see Table 1.1). This is probably related to the fact that "the Catalan nation is prior to the Spanish state, the present configuration of which is certainly the result of a long historical but essentially coercive process that has imposed political unity without creating a feeling of national unity."[62] It should also be noted that the feeling of belonging to Catalonia has increased as democracy has advanced in Spain.[63]

In Scotland, a nation that, like Catalonia, is part of a unitary political structure, people have composite identities. In 2005, 23 per cent of the people surveyed defined themselves as solely Scottish, 38 per cent as more Scottish than British, 27 per cent as equally Scottish and British, and 4% per cent as more British than Scottish. The situation had changed very little since 1997 (see Table 1.1). It is interesting to note that there is still such a strong Scottish identity even today when the inhabitants of the region have been integrated into the United Kingdom since the eighteenth century through political and military institutions and the merchant bourgeoisie.[64] The central role played by Scots when the British Empire was expanding across the globe cannot be overlooked. It surely developed complicity between the Scottish and English over the centuries. Indeed, David Miller has established that "It is precisely this shared historical experience, together with a very substantial level of cultural exchange, that has sustained a sense of common shared nationality alongside an equally powerful sense of difference."[65]

In the case of Québec, the feeling of identity has evolved through constitutional crises that have marked Canadian political life. In the last decade, the number of people reporting a uniquely Québécois identity has been growing and has reached almost one-fifth of the population. In addition, 32 per cent of the people surveyed said they were more Québécois than Canadian, while 35 per cent said they were equally Québécois and Canadian. In 2005, only 7 per cent of respondents said they felt solely Canadian, which was a historical low (see Table 1.1). The Québécois often feel dissatisfied in the Canadian federation and have a tendency to detach themselves emotionally from Canada. Among young people, this is very pronounced, as has been confirmed in work on trends in support for sovereignty in Québec by Simon Langlois and Gilles Gagné.[66]

Table 1.1 Dual identity in Catalonia, Scotland and Québec (1997–2005)

	Catalonia 1998	Catalonia 2005	Québec 1998	Québec 2005	Scotland 1997	Scotland 2005
Only*	11.5	14.5	12.0	19.0	23.0	32.0
More* than**	23.4	23.4	31.0	32.0	38.0	32.0
As* as**	43.1	44.8	32.0	35.0	27.0	22.0
More** than*	7.6	8.2	17.0	7.0	4.0	4.0
Only**	13.0	7.7	5.0	6.0	4.0	5.0
Do not know or no answer	1.4	1.6	3.0	2.0	4.0	5.0

Source: Moreno *et al.*, 1998; (the numbers come from a CROP survey for *The Gazette* between 27 March and 1 April, 1998); Sondage Léger Marketing, *The Globe and Mail*, *Le Devoir*, *Sondage Québécois*, news release available at http://legermarketing. com/documents/spclm/050427fr.pdf; Scottish Social Attitudes Surveys (National Centre for Social Research), www.natcen.ac.uk/natcen/pages/or_socialattitudes. htm#ssa.

Notes
* = Catalan, Québécois, Scottish.
** = Spanish, Canadian, British.

We could discuss the reasons for dual belonging in these three countries at great length, but what should be highlighted is that a minimum requirement for the political and community-based unity of Spain, the United Kingdom and Canada is recognition and renewal of national diversity. According to communitarian philosophers such as Charles Taylor, the challenge facing contemporary countries that have a high level of diversity is to combine political unity with national diversity and, at the same time, in Jean-Marc Ferry's words, "reconcile the universality of the legal framework with the singularity of cultural identities".[67]

The Catalans and Québécois are aware of having their own identities, though they may be plural and differentiated. Their identities are prior to the creation of the Spanish and Canadian states, and have changed over time. Indeed, as I have illustrated throughout this chapter, memory and history are essential both for constructing identity and affirming nationality. These features give meaning to the claims of national communities.

Discourse on the nation, particularly in the West, has focused on values inherited from the French Enlightenment, particularly freedom, tolerance, equality and the division of powers (Rousseau, Montesquieu). However, we also need to take into account values associated with the Scottish Enlightenment (Adam Smith, Adam Ferguson, David Hume). In many respects, Catalonia and Québec see themselves in the values promoted by Scottish Enlightenment thinkers, for example, in both of these region-states, free speech, free trade, cultural freedom, freedom of religion, independence of the legal system and individual autonomy are promoted. Perhaps we should point out a tendency that Adam Ferguson thought should be noted and that applies particularly well to Scots, Catalans and even to the Québécois: the idea that people have a marked tendency to disagree and that life in society leads to the greatest passions and greatest tensions. However, both Enlightenment movements agree that absolutism in all its forms must be eliminated.

In the twentieth century, the Catalans rose up against Franco's dictatorship and denounced the homogenizing policies established by the central government under the various regimes. The Québécois have also denounced the injustices they suffered in the long distant past at the time of the 1837–1838 Rebellions and more recently when the Constitution of Canada was patriated from Great Britain in 1981–1982.

If, as James Tully notes in the Canadian case, a

> constitution should be seen as a form of activity, an intercultural dialogue in which the culturally diverse sovereign citizens of contemporary societies negotiate agreements on their forms of association over time in accordance with the three conventions of mutual recognition, consent and cultural community,[68]

the Constitution of Canada is defective because it breaks with every one of these three constitutional conventions. It is extraordinary to see that Canadian political leaders have abandoned the original founding pact to give new foundations to the Constitution that show no regard for the history that shaped it.

Catalan and Québécois nationalism is all the more legitimate because it promotes a sharing of institutions, defends democratic and liberal values, is based on a shared history, fosters a strong common public culture and proposes an inclusive form of citizenship that takes into account the contributions of immigrants by involving them in the renewal of the nation and its underlying institutions.[69]

Québec and Catalonia have much in common: they both contain national communities with histories that show quests for cultural and national affirmation that have been as enduring as they are justified. It is this long history, in which there have been many conflicts over how to understand the political undertakings, memory and feeling of nationhood that legitimize political claims for recognition as a nation in the full sense, that has led Québec and Catalonia to portray themselves as national communities based on the principles of both communitarian and procedural liberalism.

According to Ernest Renan, a nation is both an expression of a common undertaking and the result of an historical process.[70] A nation's objectives are inspired by the inclusion of citizens in a common project in order to strengthen solidarity. In a way, establishment of an ethical political endeavour has won the support of Catalans and Québécois. This is essential because their futures as liberal societies depend on it.

I will conclude this chapter by quoting the words of the *Conseil des communautés culturelles et de l'immigration du Québec*, which established in short that "being Québécois means being de facto involved in the societal choices of Québec".[71] Being Catalan also means playing an active role in the societal choices of the national community in relation to a shared history,[72] a plural identity and an increasingly shared language. Language is thus at the heart of the political undertaking and leads to a tolerant and inclusive approach to nationalism. As the reference to Charles Taylor's work showed at the beginning of the chapter, this would enable every individual to have a horizon of meaning with its source in a feeling of belonging, allegiances and cultural traditions that enables him or her to exchange ideas in an ordinary language that is his or her own.[73] As we will see in the next chapter, this form of construction of identity operates better in the context of institutional foundations open to full recognition of national minorities within larger political bodies. We will also see how federalism offers national minorities promising avenues for cohabitation and enables different communities to express their expectations in the framework of democratic deliberation.

2 The normative foundations of asymmetrical federalism

The Canadian situation from a comparative perspective[1]

Over the years, a number of authors have proposed developing political agreements to maintain stability in pluralist societies, but few have studied the need for justice in such societies. However, I consider that the objectives of political elites should never be limited to political stability, as we are too often reminded by the sad fate of peoples that lack a democratic framework.

In this chapter, special attention will be paid to the notion of justice as it applies in democratically advanced federal states. In order to avoid straying from the topic, I will focus on federations that have been formed out of sociologically diverse political entities.[2] Thus, I will not discuss mononational or territorial federations owing to their homogeneity.

Two areas of research will be combined to understand (federal) pluralist societies: comparative politics and political theory. However, to begin with, a few warnings are required. First, there is a well-known tendency in comparative politics to place the accent on homogeneity and to presume that the inhabitants of a given city share the same opinions, speak the same language and have the same ancestors.[3] This has led a number of specialists of comparative politics to associate homogeneity with stability in political regimes. An excellent illustration of this dominant vision can be seen in the work by Alvin Rabushka and Kenneth A. Shepsle. According to them, the stability of a democracy cannot be maintained if there is cultural diversity,[4] and it is a mistake to think otherwise. Yet, a large corpus of research was nonetheless produced in the 1970s and 1980s around the notion of consociational democracy, which refers to political agreements based on a broad coalition, segmented independence for communities, proportional representation and a veto for minorities. The research looked at ways of accommodating diversity and maintaining political stability in a fair way. The most influential work in this area is that of Arend Lijphart[5] and Kenneth McRae.[6]

In political theory in the western world, there is a clear prejudice in favour of procedural liberalism. The analyst who is most representative of this is Chandran Kukathas, who posits three central principles of liberalism:

1   liberal theory is *individualistic* because it affirms or presumes the individual's moral primacy in relation to the claims of any social group;
2   it is *egalitarian* because it gives the same moral status to all individuals and denies the worth of a legal or political regime that differentiates between moral values;
3   it is *universalist* because it postulates the moral unity of the human race, thus overlooking the role of any other form of cultural expression.[7]

In the last 15 years, a number of writers have challenged the traditional reading of liberalism on the grounds that it is too restrictive. The most well-known of these critics include Iris Marion Young (1990), Will Kymlicka (1995), James Tully (1995) and Ferran Requejo (1999). They have all looked at liberalism's capacity to take into consideration "deep diversity"[8] and have proposed updating the conventional principles of liberalism so as to better understand the contemporary world.

The present political situation, particularly with respect to federal democratic societies, challenges the foundations of comparative politics and political theory, especially regarding homogeneity and individualism. Expressions of group loyalty and cultural affirmation of political communities in federal societies show that individualism and homogeneity cannot fully describe or provide complete understanding of modern political phenomena.

The capacity of federal systems to accommodate diversity in countries and provide means for nations to co-exist has been the subject of in-depth studies throughout the world, but primarily in advanced liberal democracies. Moreover, the federal system seems to be spreading into countries, such as Belgium and Spain, that are seeking to strengthen democratic practices and into countries, such as Ethiopia and Iraq, where a transition to democracy is desired.

A promising avenue for the study of comparative federalism is asymmetrical federalism, which is one of the central themes studied closely by the International Political Science Association's Comparative Federalism and Federation Research Committee. It is a propitious means of managing long-term political conflicts in federal countries, especially in those with recognized democratic traditions. Most of the work in this area concentrates on institutional aspects of establishing asymmetry in federal systems.[9]

So far, there has been little discussion of the values and ideologies – Charles de Montesquieu's "human passions" – inherent to asymmetrical federalism. While material and structural interests are essential to understanding the forces involved in developing constitutional policies, a significant part of political thought has to explore various hypotheses about what is good or valid for a society. Too often, authors relegate this dimension, which I call normative, to a level of secondary importance.

In this chapter, I will compare the various normative arguments that are used in Québec and Canada (but could easily be applied to Catalonia and Spain or Wallonia and Belgium) to support different conceptions of asymmetrical federalism, and explore the nature of the underlying value system. My objective is to show that endorsement of and opposition to asymmetrical federalism is not simply a question of pragmatism in the sense that it can be justified to grasp power or prevent secession directly, but rather that such attitudes to asymmetrical federalism are normative and embody different conceptions of the Good.

Three normative explanations for asymmetrical federalism are described below. First, I look at the communitarian conception of the Good, which is based on the fact that people do not initially act as individuals, since an individual is the product of a specific political community and history. From this point of view, states should be organized so as to protect communities, which requires an asymmetrical structure in a plural state. In Québec's case, asymmetry is justified because it provides better protection for the community defined in terms of language, culture, institutions and shared goals. Thus, asymmetrical federalism can be associated with the minority national community's importance as a source of culture. In other words, since Québec is the primary source of culture for the Québécois, the Government of Québec should have more power than a political entity that is simply a subdivision of a vast cultural entity. This communitarian justification of asymmetry clearly implies a policy of recognition, and rejects, for example, blanket enforcement of the (pan-) Canadian Charter of Rights and Freedoms on all member states of the Canadian federation (see Chapter 4) since it could undermine the basis of meaning of some communities.

A second normative explanation for the establishment of asymmetrical practices involves taking a deeper view of the classical-liberal conception of citizens' equality. Given that non-territorial federalism leads member states to legislate in specific ways in areas under provincial jurisdiction and that the citizens of a single country can receive special services and be treated differently from one member-state to the next, then it is clear that asymmetrical federalism is simply complementary. In such a context, the notion of citizenship fosters equitable (instead of equal) treatment of communities and, by extension, of individuals. The goal here is equal results, not identical treatment. The latter is embodied in what the Spanish often refer to as government policies based on the principle of *café para todos*, which might project an image of equity but are only a means of attenuating the roles of historical nations in the construction of contemporary Spain.

A third normative explanation resides less in protection of distinct cultures than in the need to strengthen the conditions for expansion of the democratic framework. The idea consists in generating conditions that favour long-term shared public debate. This kind of goal is more easily achieved in well-circumscribed cultural communities, which is a modern description of what Montesquieu called "small republics". Here again, asymmetrical federalism is interpreted as providing a means of fully achieving a pluralist, democratic federal framework.

Each of these three conceptions contains a normative explanation of asymmetrical federalism that leads to important conclusions specific to each society, such as different interpretations of the good life. We need to look at the notion of asymmetry in greater detail to see whether it can better serve the purposes of modern federal polities. However, we first have to make a distinction between the concepts of mononational and multinational federal societies. This chapter focuses essentially on the latter.

Clarification of concepts

Specialists of federalism do not always stop to define the concepts with which they work, and take it for granted that they have already been understood. However, this can result in deep misunderstanding of the subject matter. Indeed, work on federalism has been disproportionately influenced by the dominant American idea that all other types of federalism are exceptions to the rule. The dominant image of federalism in comparative politics has thus been defined in territorial terms, making the United States the prime example. But what about

Belgium, Canada, Switzerland and, recently, Spain, which seems to be taking steps towards federalism? Often the federal formula as imagined in these countries does not correspond to the territorial model promoted by Americans, though in some cases, such as in Canada and Spain, the majority group may endorse the American model.

Mononational federations, such as Australia, Germany and the United States, tend to be more stable, but their societal challenges seem smaller than those facing emerging multinational federations, such as Canada, India and Spain. However, this is a surface reading, for in Germany and the United States, the growing presence of Turkish and Hispanic groups should soon have significant impact on education, social integration and labour-market access policies in large urban centres.[10]

Juan Linz raises an interesting point with respect to democratic federations when he breaks federal states into two groups. First, there are those with the primary objective of uniting separate political entities in a single political whole (this is an essentially territorial *qua* mononational definition) and, second, those with the primary objective of maintaining political entities with specific linguistic, religious, cultural or national concentrations (this is an essentially multinational definition). The clearest examples of mononational federalism include Australia, Austria after 1918, Germany after 1821 and the United States. Those falling into the multinational federalism category include Belgium, Canada, India and Spain. Linz considers Switzerland to be a mononational country because its citizens identify themselves first with the federation as a whole, rather than with a specific canton.[11]

Examples of mononational federalism are not particularly relevant here because cultural pluralism is not a major issue for them and the notion of asymmetrical federalism is rarely invoked. Indeed, the traditional framework of democratic liberalism sees asymmetrical federalism as an aberration and some political players view it as something that must be contained.[12] References to asymmetrical federalism are normally limited to targeted studies of member states, their relative economies and their respective political influence. Researchers tend to focus more on form than on content. In multinational federalism, the stakes are not the same because member states place the accent on competing definitions of the good life. With respect to the United States, Ferran Requejo rightly states:

> If we remain within the orbit of American federalism, the answer
> to the question about the possibilities of regulating democratic

citizenship in plurinational societies is basically a negative one [...]. It is fundamentally a "territorial" model, and one that is governed by homogenizing interpretations of the democratic concept of "popular sovereignty" – which avoids the basic question, unanswered in democratic theory, about who the people are, and who decides who they are – as well as ideas about equality of citizenship and equality between the federated units.[13]

Questions relating to equal citizenship and equality among federated entities are particularly useful for analysing asymmetrical federalism. There are a number of forms of asymmetry but only political and constitutional asymmetries have direct consequences for political communities. Differences among members of a federation, in terms of land size, population and wealth, play a role in the exercise of power, but the division of powers and sovereignty is what is most important.

An asymmetrical federal structure requires that a country's federal nature be embedded in the Constitution and weighted by the division of powers between the central and regional governments or by the composition of central decision-making institutions, and that member states have to have different relations with the central government and its jurisdiction, institutions and laws.[14] By insisting on constitutional entrenchment, this definition excludes de facto asymmetrical arrangements[15] resulting from special features specific to a group, distinct cultural traditions, different economic activities and specific political choices. Below I will look at asymmetrical federalism, paying special attention to the exercise of various member states' powers, but without examining supranational forms of federalism.

In Canada, asymmetrical agreements between the provinces and the central government have characterized the federation's development owing to the various goals and objectives of the constituent states. With the Quiet Revolution[16] that transformed Québec in the 1960s, and the deep ideological changes that accompanied it, Québec's demands for constitutional recognition as distinct from the other provinces began to increase significantly. In the wake of the Quiet Revolution, Ottawa's first concrete official recognition of cultural duality was in the 1968 Laurendeau–Dunton Commission Report, which defined it clearly as a fundamental constitutive principle of the Canadian state. The central government subsequently sought to limit the Report's influence to federal institutions by challenging the leadership role that Québec had until then played in relation to French Canadians.

Demands from the Québec government for asymmetrical decentralization of powers have often been perceived outside Québec as a potential threat to the survival of the federation, thus casting suspicion on requests for "asymmetrical federalism". Among Canadians outside Québec, asymmetrical federalism has come to be seen as only a strategic manoeuvre on the part of the Québec elite to obtain greater power. Nonetheless, the fact that there is de facto asymmetry in the Canadian federation in terms of administrative agreements and geographical and demographic features has often been noted[17] and has helped to legitimize some claims to *de jure* asymmetry by the Québécois and First Nations. In the past, people have suggested promoting asymmetry as a means of solving the long-standing Canadian constitutional crisis. In particular, this was one of the conclusions of the Citizen's Forum on Canada's Future in 1991, which was held in the context of a pan-Canadian consultation leading up to the failed Charlottetown Accord.[18] In the Forum's report, it was noted:

> Given that provinces have entered confederation on different terms and operate under different provisions, we believe that special arrangements in provinces based on special needs *are a fundamental principle of Canadian federalism*. This principle would apply where needed to all provinces.[19]

The authors of the report continue by asserting that Canadians should "place the emphasis on equity in the face of specific needs" and accept that "Québec should have the freedom and means to be itself – a unique society with its own distinctive place in a renewed Canadian family".[20] These ideas are familiar to Basques, Catalans and Galicians in the new Spain, that of autonomies.

Asymmetrical federalism is praised by some authors because it reduces the potential for secession. Will Kymlicka's work[21] supports our reading of this phenomenon by establishing that when communities are autonomous, minority communities have real foundations on which they can rest to project themselves into the future without adopting foreign forms. Federalism thus becomes an honourable means of management for every partner in a federation, and a means of not breaking the constitutional pact that originally brought the entities together.

Reginald Whitaker has, however, pointed out that the popularity of asymmetrical federalism among English-speaking Canadians tends to drop as the threat of Québec sovereignty dissipates.[22] It is as if asymmetrical federalism can be taken seriously only when secession is seen as the last resort by political players. Asymmetrical federalism certainly offers new possibilities for managing conflicts between communities that every democratic state should hasten to investigate fully. Yet, political players often stubbornly dig themselves into irreconcilable positions that cut off all ways out of the crisis. Too often such political players grapple with one another with an "all or nothing" attitude, the consequence of which is to exclude more conciliatory solutions. Thus, unless there is unassailable national solidarity,[23] might will be right, and the central power will prevail.

While pragmatic visions of asymmetrical federalism, as sketched above, contain a normative dimension, they are different from the more universal categories of values and ideologies mentioned at the beginning of this chapter because they do not directly ask the question: "What is good for a given society?" In comparison with normative considerations, justifications such as administrative efficiency, performance[24] and national unity taken as an end in itself are less important. Let us look now at the first of these normative categories: the communitarian principle.

The communitarian principle

The first normative explanation invoked to promote the adoption of asymmetrical federalism comes from the community's importance for life in society. In response to the question, "What is fundamentally good for a given society?" we should expect an answer based on normative values such as "our community, our culture, our identity and our heritage".

All people are fundamentally social beings who need cultural baggage, such as symbols and a living language, that can be used in all aspects of social relations and to strengthen the feeling of belonging and identity. Life in society requires that the culture of political communities flourish and that such communities are protected and promoted by the state so as to ensure their long-term continuity.[25] From this point of view, if a government provides leadership on behalf of a political community, it should be invested with powers appropriate for setting up public policy to sustain the community.

Defence of community has its origins in Greek philosophy and was already a political idea in the Middle Ages. In the seventeenth and eighteenth centuries, European philosophers, such as Johan Althusius and Montesquieu, renewed the tradition in reaction to absolutist notions of sovereignty that were current at the time and in order to reply to the centralizing desires of monarchies. At the time of the

American Federal Convention of 1787, the establishment of a decentralized structure in the Constitution was defended by those who idealized small communities as a form of social organization and wanted to create a political structure for the colonies that corresponded to the idea of a small, pastoral republic. While the Anti-Federalists, as they were strangely called, lost their quest for sovereignty at the state level, a number of authors have suggested that their position influenced the federal structure that was finally adopted by the United States of America.[26]

In Canada, the adoption of a federal structure at the time of the British North America Act in 1867 was praised, especially by political leaders and Catholic clergy in Québec. It was seen as a bulwark to protect the religion, language, and legal and educational institutions of the new province of Québec. Studying this period, Samuel V. LaSelva notes that, at the time, "The Canadian tension relates not to liberty but to identity and to the relation (or clash) between local identities and national identity. [...] Canada was to be a nation in which multiple loyalties and multiple identities flourished."[27]

This understanding of Canadian federalism as resting on multiple identities drew many converts throughout the country, though it has been undermined since its creation by proponents of a unitary approach. Moreover, at the beginning of the twentieth century, the Autonomists, led by the former Premier of Ontario, Oliver Mowat, opposed the imposition of "National, uniform standards on culturally, religiously, and linguistically distinct provinces".[28] The Autonomist position was a big success in Québec, where there was a strong concentration of the French Canadian nation at the origin of the federal pact.[29]

For partisans of a "special" constitutional status for Québec, expression of federalism's *bias* in favour of the community is a very positive development. It has often been concluded that Québec should be recognized as a nation in the Constitution because that would convey a fundamental reality of the Canadian federation: allegiance and identity in Québec are different from those prevailing in the rest of Canada. The notion of a distinct society can be understood from the angle of deeply anchored symbols, and its contribution to building a feeling of a political community is significant.

A more concrete argument in favour of asymmetrical federalism resides in the fact that there is a notion of a public good specific to Québec and foreign to the other Canadian provinces, namely, the moral obligation to protect and promote the French language and culture in North America. Indeed, Québec is the only jurisdiction in

North America where French-speakers form a majority. The Government of Québec thus seeks to be mandated with responsibilities that are beyond those of other member states of the federation because it can defend the interests of the Québec nation, French-speaking minorities outside Québec and the Francophonie in North America.[30] According to Fernand Dumont, the issue is equivalent to the state's necessary role in protecting nations in a given area. He says that "If it is the state's responsibility to promote equality among citizens and to foster distributive justice, that responsibility concerns in particular the maintenance and full development of national communities."[31]

Arguments in favour of setting up asymmetrical public policies designed to protect and promote Québec culture can also be based on historical continuity. Here we are arguing that it serves the common good to preserve the language, traditions, institutions and symbols of earlier generations, and members of the political community. Catalonia, Wales and Québec have to act not only as the inheritors but also as the guardians of cultures and political legacies.

The Spanish Constitution of 1978 asserts the importance of maintaining such continuity; it makes it a question of solidarity. The Preamble stipulates that the purpose of the Constitution is to "protect all Spaniards and peoples of Spain in the exercise of human rights, their cultures and traditions, languages, and institutions". In Article 3, the Constitution also sets out that "The richness of the linguistic modalities of Spain is a cultural patrimony which will be the object of special respect and protection." This relationship to history is crucial in that it enables both citizens in general and members of national historical communities in particular to situate their experiences in a context and at the same time imagine their future.

In Canada, James Tully is certainly the researcher who has made the greatest contribution to the study of constitutional policy by focusing specifically on the discourse proper to historical continuity. Inspired by the major principles of contemporary liberalism, Tully shows that a federal relationship between governments can resemble relationships between individuals. Like individuals who have a culture of rights, duties and responsibilities, governments are linked with their counterparts in their relations. Such solidarity is essential to building and maintaining trust. Tully identifies three conventions that translate the federal spirit, namely, mutual recognition, continuity and consent, which are the foundations of constitutionalism.[32]

According to Tully, the division of powers between the federal government and provincial governments as set out in the British North America Act was established in accordance with the two first conventions: recognition of the culture of member states of the Confederation and continuity of those cultures in the new constitutional framework. In Québec's case, the culture of Lower Canada was recognized, preserved and perpetuated by the Civil Code, property rights, and maintenance of the French language, customs and religion. He argues that consistency with the three conventions can legitimize claims in favour of asymmetry if powers under the jurisdiction of the member states are later centralized.[33]

The decision of the central government (in conjunction with the nine English-speaking provinces) to break with the three constitutional conventions by patriating the Constitution in 1981–1982 without Québec's consent undermined, to use Arend Lijphart's description, the overarching loyalties between Québec and the rest of Canada. This thus eroded federal loyalty (i.e. *Bundestreue* in German) since it put an end to the constitutional practice that had until then required Québec's support for all significant constitutional amendments.[34]

The first category of normative arguments in favour of asymmetrical federalism focuses on the importance of national groups as conduits for culture. What about individuals? Can we protect individuals but at the same time promote collective rights? This is the central theme of the next section.

The egalitarian principle

The second category of values underlying defence of asymmetrical federalism lies in the expression of equality between peoples and requires that special attention be paid to liberty, equality and justice so as to better identify the three-way relationship among groups, individuals and the state. The features that are most often highlighted in this debate concern issues around the meaning of citizenship and nature of egalitarian treatment of individuals. Detractors of asymmetrical federalism hold that it could lead to imbalances and unfair practices, thereby creating a second-class status for individuals who do not consider themselves full members of the political community and are sometimes ready to mount passionate opposition.

In Canada's case, Alan C. Cairns is of the opinion that asymmetrical application of the Canadian Charter of Rights and Freedoms could lead to the establishment of asymmetrical citizenship and, by extension, cause problems with respect to individuals' allegiance to nation building.[35] This interpretation is based essentially on a monist normative model applying to a set of values and rights embedded in a constitution, unshared sovereignty and transcendent nationality. Should not contemporary challenges invite us to go beyond this reading to propose a new vision that is more sensitive to the various contributions of the communities at the origin of states and gives them a greater role to play in, for example, international organizations and supranational institutions? Could not the United Nations Educational, Scientific and Cultural Organization (UNESCO), World Trade Organization (WTO), World Health Organization (WHO) and International Labour Organization (ILO) reformulate their membership policies to allow national minorities to join?

Here we suggest that adopting an alternative normative discourse that holds that Canada is composed of a set of distinct political communities would also defend a vision of Canadian citizenship according to which all Canadians are equal. From this point of view, there is no conflict or rivalry between citizenship and allegiance to a federal political community. An illustration of this is Spain, where autonomous communities and *a fortiori* historical national communities are completely legitimate participants in the construction of a federal Spain.[36]

Richard Vernon asserts that the citizens of truly federal states are *federated citizens* in the sense that their loyalty is divided between levels of government, each of which is sovereign in its jurisdiction. In a way, what is in question is a means for citizens to take full advantage of their multiple identities. Citing Pierre Joseph Proudhon favourably, Vernon suggests that to "the extent that 'the federal principle' leaves open the question of priority, permitting individuals to balance one attachment against another, it permits more scope".[37] Various conceptions of citizenship co-exist in federal and multinational democratic regimes, and they should be supported as long as they meet liberal requirements on the equality of citizens in each of the federation's member states.

Federalism, particularly multinational federalism, supposes that people living in different member states can be subject to different laws. Reginald Whitaker even goes so far as to say that "Modern federalism is an institutionalisation of the formal limitation of the national majority will as the legitimate ground for legislation."[38] Owing to the rules by which federal systems function, the voice of the national majority cannot be an efficient expression of the sovereignty of the people. This problem has largely been resolved by federalist theory, and specialists of federalism have rapidly come to accept the legitimacy of shared sovereignty in federations.

Asymmetrical federalism follows the same trajectory as symmetrical federalism in its conceptualization of citizens' equality that is inspired by the unitary (i.e. standardizing)[39] model of the state according to which the law treats all in the same way. However, it takes the reasoning a little further: it accepts that differences in jurisdiction and laws are completely appropriate for member states of a federation.

Federalism is a means of taking the concept of equality beyond the restrictive interpretation of equal treatment and substituting a more subtle interpretation of equal opportunity or even overall equality among national communities. In this way, various positive measures for establishing greater equality among groups have been proposed as means of eliminating traditional obstacles. Once situated in the historical, social and economic context, such measures are easy to justify in that they are there to correct unfair situations.

According to James Tully, it is important to make a distinction between identical treatment and equitable treatment when the principle of equality is in question. He says that legal monism corresponds to the former, while modern pluralism is related to the latter.[40] Similarly, procedural liberalism is typically monist, while communitarian liberalism is related to pluralism. Asymmetrical federalism is often cited as a tool for achieving equity rather than strict equality, and as a communitarian instrument rather than a device for procedural liberalism. From this perspective, equality between individuals and nations in a federation should be considered in accordance with their specific needs and historical development and not so much on the basis of an identical, interchangeable relationship with other individuals or other member states.

In recent years, a number of studies on Canadian and Spanish politics have highlighted the importance of egality and equity in debates around asymmetrical federalism's role in improving the operation of political institutions. For example, in *Canada: Reclaiming the Middle Ground*, Donald Lenihan, Gordon Robertson and Roger Tassé argue that Canada has to deal with the different conceptions of procedural and communitarian liberalism that generally characterize multinational federal states.[41] The political questions about what separates individuals and their communities (and their collective rights) and how such rights should be evaluated reveal a profound socio-cultural dimension and have to be assessed in relation to different cultural contexts.

While classical liberalism imposes formal equality on all citizens, Lenihan and his colleagues assert that this does not take into account the very different consequences that equal treatment can have for different regions and different nations with respect to the implementation of government policies. The quest for equal treatment should not prevent us from attaining egality at the level of results.[42] This is all the more pertinent when what is in question is maintaining the equality of member states in a given multinational federation despite social, economic and cultural differences. Lenihan, Robertson and Tassé write:

> The claim that provincial equality implies sameness of treatment is open to the same kind of objection raised against a formal approach to the equality of persons. Those who argue this way seem to confuse the (sound) claim that the federal government should treat the interests of all provinces with equal concern and respect with the (unsound) claim that all provinces should be treated the same. This ignores the fact that provinces (like individuals) sometimes have special needs or may be burdened by circumstances.[43]

The question of equality of results becomes more complex when we take into account the nature of the laws and rights that are used specifically to define it. The distinction between individual and collective rights dates back to Antiquity, but it still remains very pertinent. A number of authors have suggested that the tensions between Québec and Canada, like those between Catalonia and Spain and between Scotland and the United Kingdom, flow from different approaches to recognition of rights. Thus, while English Canada is more familiar with individual rights, the Québécois focus on collective rights to improve individual rights. The same holds for all three examples.

André Burelle argues that Canada's political dilemma flows from the Canadian government's inability to recognize the different values that mould Québec society. He describes the irreconcilable values as the Québec people's *right to difference*, and invites the Québécois and Canadians outside Québec to meet halfway to find common ground. According to Burelle, those who insist that the distinct value structure should be maintained in Québec also have to be ready to accept the need to maintain the social and economic union in Canada and permit the central government to play a major role in that area. In turn, those who support only individual rights have to recognize and guarantee that the Québec government has the tools it needs to assert its right to difference.[44]

Among such tools, the Canadian Charter of Rights and Freedoms should not be imposed on a pan-Canadian scale, according to authors such as James Tully, without there first being respect for the fact that the country developed on the basis of agreements and out of different cultures.[45] This interpretation is shared by the great majority of political theorists in Québec. One of the most influential spokespersons on the topic is Guy Laforest who has not hesitated to say that former Prime Minister Pierre Elliott Trudeau used the Canadian Charter of Rights and Freedoms as an instrument of "typically English–Canadian nationalism" and thus tried to establish a Canadian nation without paying attention to the Québec nation. Noting the Prime Minister's power to unilaterally appoint judges not only to the Supreme Court of Canada but also to the provincial superior courts, Laforest shows that "the Charter, through the judicialization of the political system, works against Canada's federal nature. Judicial authority is the power that least reflects the federal reality of our country."[46] In order to correct the situation, we could initially imagine a political solution that would require asymmetrical application of the Canadian Charter of Rights and Freedoms such that Québec and Aboriginal communities are not subject to the homogenizing tendency flowing from it.

Until now, it has been put forth that the normative arguments underlying asymmetrical federalism in multinational democratic federations can be attributed to general principles relating to community and the search for equality. The third and last principle, which is the most important of all, is related to strengthening democratic practices.

The democratic principle

In response to the question, "What is fundamentally good for a society?" those who use normative arguments in favour of asymmetrical federalism answer: democratic expression of citizenship. In Canada, it is frequently argued that asymmetrical federalism strengthens the democratic system in that it encourages popular participation in decision-making processes and seeks to accommodate differences among political parties. This strengthens the democratic legitimacy of the federal state. In contrast, partisans of the territorial vision of federalism maintain that the traditional notions of national citizenship could be threatened if we have to commit ourselves further in that direction.[47]

A normative argument in favour of the federal avenue suggests that federalism maximizes individuals' public participation, and that this is for the well-being of democratic life in society. Jeffrey Spinner points out that

> The liberal state should work toward ensuring that all of its citizens are fluent in the public language. [...] Deny ethnic children

knowledge of the dominant language and they will undoubtedly retain many aspects of the ethnic culture – and remain economically subordinate. Allophones in Quebec who want to preserve all of the elements of their culture by preventing their children from learning French well and encouraging them to remain fluent in their native language are condemning their children to lives of obstructed economic opportunities.[48]

From this perspective, under federalism, individuals are more interested in and better informed about issues that specifically concern their political community, region and locality. They are more likely to understand local problems and hold elected representatives accountable for their actions. Provincial or state public servants are directly accountable and answerable to the people, while the central government takes care of policy said to be in the common interest.

It is easy to trace this argument in favour of federalism back to Baron de Montesquieu. A number of passages in *The Spirit of Laws* are devoted to the value of small republics, which, he argues, guarantee citizens' freedom. Montesquieu acknowledges that an individual does not act only as a separate entity but also as a member of a cultural group, society, people and nation. The culture of a people, which Montesquieu refers to as the General Spirit, is marked "by the climate, by the religion, by the laws, by the maxims of government, by precedents, morals and customs".[49] Today, we link identity with the political community. The general spirit guides the civic action of individuals; likewise, in the political dimension, "public goods" can be identified that are based on the general spirit. Montesquieu holds that the laws that govern individuals should be in accordance with the spirit of the culture of the people and designed to achieve the public good that is specific to the community in question.[50]

According to Montesquieu, the citizen of a small republic has a greater feeling of belonging to that republic than he or she could feel towards a larger, more distant state. Consequently, popular sovereignty is better protected in a small republic. Montesquieu's writings reveal, however, that he was also interested in the advantages of uniting small republics. According to him, large monarchies are better able to defend their territory and maintain international relations than are small republics, and, moreover, small republics require a compromise in terms of freedom and autonomy.[51] Montesquieu considered the federal system of government to be a solution to the perpetual dichotomy between the competing values of freedom and authority.

A similar theory can also be found in the writings of Pierre Joseph Proudhon, a nineteenth-century French theorist who wrote that small and local governments were always more likely to act as ramparts against abuses of power than were large governments. Highly centralized bureaucracy, which is necessary to regulate some aspects of social life, erodes citizens' freedom by distancing them from popular sovereignty. Proudhon held that the federal principle should be seen as a balance between the competing concepts of authority and freedom: central government provides the former while regional government delivers the latter.[52]

The desire to protect freedom by guaranteeing local sovereignty, as expressed by Montesquieu and Proudhon, is entirely related to the concept of political community and makes it possible to legitimize the establishment of asymmetrical federalism. According to Jeremy Webber, all political communities are structured in accordance with a common language that serves as a framework for public debate and makes it possible to develop a general consensus around objectives and allegiances in the community. He says that "[w]hen Canadians follow a political debate, they are usually following the version that occurs in their public language. When they care about the outcome of that debate, they do so in terms relating to the discussion they know."[53] In short, languages can cut across political communities, but the opposite is not true.[54]

The language of each community is also imposed when a constitution is interpreted in a multinational federal framework. In his study on Spain, Ferran Requejo says that, contrary to the generally held opinion according to which the government is neutral in democratic liberal societies, the reality is very different. He shows that

> Apart from recognizing the rights of citizenship, liberal institutions introduce a whole range of hegemonic linguistic and cultural traits and values in the public sphere in order to create a homogeneous "national" identity from above [...].
>
> [The normative foundations of the liberal-democratic rights and rules] have never been "neutral" as far as individual identities are concerned, because those rights and rules include a whole range of implicit *particularist* cultural values (such as language, reconstruction of history, "common" traditions etc.) which go beyond mere procedural and universalist issues.[55]

The absence of neutrality resulting from the expression of rights and dominant rules in multinational federal states once again shows the need to implement asymmetrical federalism. Charles Taylor's analysis is particularly pertinent here. As we saw at the beginning of this chapter, according to Taylor, the challenge facing multinational states lies in recognition of deep diversity. He warns:

> To build a country for everyone, Canada would have to allow for second-level or "deep" diversity, in which a plurality of ways of belonging would also be acknowledged and accepted. Someone of, say, Italian extraction in Toronto or Ukrainian extraction in Edmonton might indeed feel Canadian as a bearer of individual rights in a multicultural mosaic. His or her belonging would not "pass through" some other community, although the ethnic identity might be important to him or her in various ways. But this person might nevertheless accept that a Québécois or a Cree or a Déné might belong in a very different way, that these persons were Canadian through being members of their national communities.[56]

Taylor also advances the idea that Canadian society is influenced by a model of participation different from that of the United States, where the focus is on individual rights alone. According to Taylor, it is essential that people respect the public institutions that determine the rules of social and political life, that they have a personal interest in the shared definition of the "good life" and that members of a multinational community have a shared identity. Canada's heterogeneity leads Taylor to conclude, however, that "we do not have and cannot develop a single national identity"[57] owing to the existence of Québec. Taylor therefore suggests major decentralization of the Canadian federation and, in cases where the jurisdictional needs and priorities of English–Canadian provinces do not correspond to those of Québec, asymmetrical federalism should be strongly promoted. Taylor's argument is completely consistent with the democratic principle because his primary concern lies in political participation, which determines and shapes cultural identity.

Subscribing to federalism, Jeremy Webber, Charles Taylor and Ferran Requejo, like other researchers who propose asymmetrical solutions for Canada[58] and Spain,[59] adopt a vision of the federal state as a *community of communities*, in which member states are the primary political expression of the general will. An additional point that should be made concerning asymmetrical federalism and the normative principles flowing from the democratic principle brings us to the issue of legitimacy. Legitimacy in a federal society depends

both on the feeling of belonging and on respect for political preferences freely expressed by the people.

The Canadian federal system suffers from a lack of legitimacy in
Québec, and this has taken on worrisome proportions since the Constitution was patriated. According to Janet Ajzenstat, "What changed
is that the 1982 act is no mere program of the federal government,
but part of the Constitution, the supreme law of the country."[60]
Ajzenstat observes that the decision to patriate the Constitution
without the consent of the Québec National Assembly severely
undermined the legitimacy of the Canadian federal system in the eyes
of the Québécois. For them, the crisis of legitimacy results from the
fact that since 1982, the dominant principles of the liberal democratic
framework have been greatly weakened.

> Procedural liberalism was said not to tolerate a prior idea of the
> good in politics – the constitution, the system of government,
> should be neutral with respect to ideology and political interest.
> The constitution is the rule book for the game of politics. The
> fact that it does not prefer one way of life, one political ideology
> or program, is what enables parties to come and go in office,
> secures respect for political opposition, and enables marginal
> groups to bid for influence. The procedural constitution is sup-
> posed to be above politics, immune to political manipulation, in
> order to make politics possible.[61]

All of that was set aside by the 1982 patriation. Now politics have
been weakened, and political actions have to take the form of legal
challenges between the nations at the origin of the Canadian experiment. Today, we find ourselves in a situation where groups (women,
environmentalists, gays, religious groups, ethnic communities, etc.)
seem to pursue a single goal: that of improving their position at the
expense of others. As Jacques Beauchemin has pointed out, we are on
the way to fully embracing the *society of identities*.[62] Often encouraged by the central government,[63] the actors in such a society seek to
impose their points of view by bypassing the democratic institutions
of national communities and elected officials. The idea of a neutral
constitution is simply abandoned. Consequently, justice in Canada
develops in accordance with the orientations of the leading political
forces, and is no longer based on the principles of constitutionalism
that originally gave meaning to the Canadian federation.[64] We are
witnessing a profound change in politics in the sense that deliberation
is short-circuited in favour of defence of identity interests enshrined

in the Charter of Rights and Freedoms. There is also now no discussion of the multinational stakes that should be central to any debate on construction of a common, shared citizenship in a multinational federation.

> Neglecting the moral foundations of federalism is unproblematic so long as the practice of federalism is accepted.[65]

We have seen that the philosophical theses and ideological positions underlying multinational democratic federal regimes can be categorized according to three general principles: the democratic principle, which is intended to guarantee an accountable government, more active political participation and greater awareness of citizenship; the community principle, which highlights the wealth of cultures, ensures historical continuity and sees to greater fairness among communities; and finally the egalitarian principle, which promotes equality and freedom. So long as the regime is consistent with these three principles, long-term political stability can be ensured.

Federalism, particularly asymmetrical federalism, is a tool that provides a wide range of solutions to the problems of multinational states.[66] In so far as the federal principle can be established as a dynamic yet flexible force conducive to creative innovation, and thus distant from some of the standardizing features of more traditional federations, it can be a powerful tool for accommodation in multinational democratic societies.[67]

As we mentioned at the beginning of this chapter, it is important today to place greater emphasis on justice, fairness and egality in order to find appropriate answers to the challenge of deep diversity. Increasingly, contemporary democratic states will have to take the multinational road (see Chapters 3, 4 and 6) if they want to be able to fulfil their obligations to the nations at their origins. There are promising experiments underway in Belgium and Spain with respect to transition from a unitary to a federal state. The 2005–2006 constitutional negotiations in Spain to give Catalonia a new autonomous status also indicate some flexibility in the political process and removal of obstacles to democracy.[68] This is an encouraging sign in view of possibly improving relations between the Spanish government and the Basque country, and also provides useful avenues to be explored by federal states that are currently little inclined to meet national minorities' demands for autonomy.

Today, Spain seems to be succeeding where Canada has failed to meet the challenge of deep diversity. In the case of Canada, the federal spirit has been shaken in recent years, and the consequences of this are yet unclear. The emerging federal Belgium could provide valuable insight because, as Francis Delpérée points out, "the most elementary form of federal loyalty is respect for the federal constitution. It is respect for the rules of the game."[69] Yet, in Canada, the decision to patriate the Constitution in 1981–1982 weakened Québécois' trust in the overall Canadian political regime because Canada broke the rules and imposed new conditions on shared life with little regard for Québec's legitimate political claims.[70] This has produced major tensions between the proponents of procedural liberalism, which is favourable to the majority national group, and those of communitarian liberalism, who wish to maintain the stability of political regimes by placing primary importance on community recognition. In the next chapter we will therefore review these two schools of thought, personified in Canada by Pierre Elliott Trudeau and Charles Taylor, respectively.

3 The emerging phenomenon of the multination[1]

John Rawls' work on liberalism has probably contributed the most to advancing the debate among Americans by establishing a link between respect for individual rights and the development of richer and more vibrant liberal democracies.[2] Rawls and many later thinkers, such as Ronald Dworkin, have focused on protecting individual rights, arguing that a procedural approach provides more equal protection for individuals, while also insisting (particularly in Rawls' case) on the idea of distribution of wealth so as to assist underprivileged groups. The contributions of American researchers are also important with respect to the recognition of social movements in the African-American and the gay and lesbian communities, as well as of the feminist movement and the struggle for employment equity (Iris Marion Young, Amy Gutmann, Nira Yuval-Davis).[3] Civil rights struggles in the United States and elsewhere in the West have been fundamental and cannot be ignored because they have qualitatively advanced our conceptions of political and social rights.

A number of Canadian philosophers have sought to set themselves apart from their Anglo-American colleagues. For example, Charles Taylor has replied to Ronald Dworkin[4] by making a distinction between procedural and substantive commitments in liberalism. Taylor's purpose is to show that a society does not stop being liberal simply because it adopts a substantive moral position, quite the contrary. Taylor defends the idea that

> A society with strong collective goals can be liberal, on this view, provided it is also capable of respecting diversity, especially when it concerns those who do not share its goals; and provided it can offer adequate safeguards for fundamental rights.[5]

Taylor's work and that of many who have followed him has given rise to very rich thought on diversity, recognition and the quest for authenticity. Today, with the benefit of hindsight, we can see that nothing less than a new school of thought has emerged that is becoming increasingly influential in universities and political circles as new states are forming in both the West and the East.

The present chapter is structured around four lines. First, we will review the vision of two nations that long characterized the relations between Québec and Canada so as to gain a better understanding of the importance of history in the construction of identity. Second, we will revisit the notion of deep diversity as developed by Charles Taylor and elaborated by his followers. Third, we will see the degree to which the philosopher Taylor and the politician Pierre Trudeau offer different visions of Canada. The former managed to gain international recognition for the reconciliatory qualities of his model, while the latter seems, for now at least, to have won the political battle in Canada and in certain states that are solely inclined to recognize individual rights. Finally, fourth, we will discuss the urgent need to move forward to a new stage, that of affirming the multination as a legitimate option by relaunching the Canadian experiment on foundations that are more democratic and, above all, more respectful of the roots of the national communities concerned. Québec's success or failure to gain acknowledgement of its national claims will be extremely important for nations said to be stateless (e.g. Catalonia, the Basque country, Scotland and Corsica) because success would open the way for the possibility of real recognition and political institutions that could meet the expectations of all national communities living with the experience of domination in multinational countries.

Dualism and pluralism

From 1867 to 1960, Québec and the rest of Canada essentially ignored one another. The "two founding peoples", as they saw themselves at the time, developed on their respective territories, initially in accordance with the underlying principles of consociational democracy.[6] Four general principles were at the foundations of that democracy: a broad coalition bringing together the various components of society, mutual veto or an effective competing majority, proportionality in allocation of resources and governance, and a high degree of autonomy so that each partner could manage its own affairs.

The golden age of consociational democracy in Canada was from 1848 to 1867, when political players were trying to combine Upper and Lower Canada into a single country. Once the Canadian Confederation was established in 1867, the general principles of consociational democracy gradually crumbled and were replaced by majority democracy that showed little regard for Québec's expectations of the Canadian federation. Political and economic factors led, over the years, to different changes in each of the above four principles.

As Canada was being built, the leading political parties on the federal scene played major, sometimes determinant, roles in taking regional claims into account.[7] The parties were much less successful when it came to answering the claims of minority nations in the Canadian federation, which led to clashes and numerous political crises over the years. The principal frictions were between English and French Canadians and, more recently, Canadians outside Québec and the Québécois. For example, the two national communities held diametrically opposing visions of the Louis Riel case, Canadian participation in the First and Second World Wars, and, more recently, patriation of the Canadian Constitution in 1982.[8]

The 1960s were marked by a willingness on the part of Canada to listen to Québec claims. Most federal political leaders at the time were amenable to mitigating the tensions in Québec–Canada relations through the idea of Canadian duality. Prime Minister Lester B. Pearson's creation of the Laurendeau–Dunton Commission in 1963, the New Democratic Party's greater awareness under the leadership of Tommy Douglas, and Robert Stanfield's Conservatives' promotion of the idea of two founding peoples in 1968, confirm that the leaders of the major political parties supported the idea of two nations. Conditions changed when Pierre Elliott Trudeau came to power and replaced Lester B. Pearson as leader of the Liberal Party of Canada in 1968. From then on, the Liberals turned their backs on Québec's demands for accommodation in the federation, and quickly rejected the Laurendeau–Dunton Commission report's conclusions on Canadian dualism.[9]

While open to defending bilingualism in federal institutions, Pierre Trudeau was always firmly opposed to recognizing duality as a foundation of political life in Canada.[10] He battled all defenders of provincial rights and all those who wanted a special status for Québec in the Canadian federation. This has been a root cause of the frictions between Québec and the rest of Canada over the last four decades.

With the avowed purpose of opposing proponents of Canadian dualism, Prime Minister Trudeau, who was in power in Ottawa from 1968 to 1979 and again from 1980 to 1984, defended individual rights and at the same time promoted multiculturalism in order to diminish as much as possible any demand for national recognition from Québec. Thus, French-speaking Québécois were portrayed as one "ethnic group" among others. There was, therefore, no question of Ottawa and the English-speaking provinces recognizing Québec as a community of belonging or of accepting Québec's demands to assert itself in its own areas of jurisdiction on the international scene, as was proposed by Paul Gérin-Lajoie, the then Minister of Education and Deputy Premier of Québec.[11]

Indeed, recent advances in multiculturalism and advent of the Canadian Charter of Rights and Freedoms have constituted a rejection of liberal communitarianism as proposed, for example, by Charles Taylor. As a new Canadian icon, the Charter[12] essentially recognizes first-degree diversity according to which Canada is made up of many cultures, each belonging to the Canadian federation in the same way. Taylor articulates this as the idea that

> [t]here are great differences in culture and outlook and background in a population that nonetheless shares the same idea of what it is to belong to Canada. Their patriotism or manner of belonging is uniform, whatever their other differences, and this is felt to be a necessity if the country is to hold together.[13]

While the rest of Canada has been pursuing its strategy of pan-Canadian integration with little regard for the claims of Québec, Québec has responded to Canadian multiculturalism and the rapid sustained advances of the procedural approach described above by developing its own model of interculturalism as a key element of its social cohesion.

Reacting to Canada's reluctance to recognize Québec on its own terms and inspired by a perceived desire to turn the residents of Québec into Québécois in their own right, the Government of Québec, civil society and intellectuals[14] have used the public sphere to debate the nature of the Québec nation and to its contributions to the development of liberal democratic states. The debates have led a number of small nations, including Wallonia, Scotland and Catalonia,[15] to cite only a few examples, to look to Québec for answers to their own problems in unitary nation-states.

Québec is thus increasingly a pluralist society with respect to ideologies and a plural society in terms of cultural composition, yet at the same time it has not renounced the hope of one day being recognized as a nation-state. This desire continues to be fed by the fact that the recognition sought by a large portion of the population of Québec has not been granted, a state of affairs that encourages sovereigntist leaders to pursue their plans for national affirmation.[16] Their demands echo Taylor's reflection on the homogenizing Canadian approach, which they denounce as dangerous for Québec's future. Thus, like Charles Taylor, we have to ask why Canadian political leaders contribute so greatly to the secessionist cause by turning their backs on Québec's primary demands rather than showing greater sensitivity,[17] as the United Kingdom has shown for Scotland, Belgium for Wallonia and France for New Caledonia.

> Instead of pushing ourselves to the point of breakup in the name of the uniform model, we would do our own and some other peoples a favour by exploring the space of deep diversity. To those who believe in according people the freedom to be themselves, this would be counted a gain in civilization. In this exploration we would not be alone. Europe-watchers have noticed how the development of the European Community has gone along with an increased breathing space for regional societies – Breton, Basque, Catalan – that were formerly threatened with the steamroller of the national state.[18]

In any case, Québec as a political power projects a positive, inspiring image for small nations seeking recognition. Yet, after 40 years of demands and commissions of inquiry of all kinds, Québec must still play the sovereigntist card in order to get the attention of its counterparts in the Canadian federation.

It is useful to note that it was the Supreme Court of Canada, in the *Reference Re. the Secession of Québec*, that put the principle of duality as a foundation of the Canadian federation back on the agenda. In paragraph 93 of the Reference, the Supreme Court ruled that if the Québécois vote "yes" to a clear question on their constitutional future, equal-to-equal negotiations must follow. This breathes new life into the formula used in the 1980 referendum. The Court requires

> the reconciliation of various rights and obligations by the representatives of two legitimate majorities, namely, the clear majority of the population of Québec, and the clear majority of Canada as a whole, whatever that be. There can be no suggestion that either of these majorities "trumps" the other.

In sum, the Supreme Court's opinion bestows obvious legitimacy upon Québec's claims and invites political players to demonstrate wisdom and restraint.

What was the Government of Canada's reaction to the Supreme Court of Canada's openness to Québec's right to renegotiate constitutional arrangements with the central government? In spring 2000, the Government of Canada rapidly adopted Bill C-20 to regain the political initiative, carefully stipulating that it alone was competent to determine whether the question posed in the next referendum was sufficiently clear, and what percentage support was required in the popular consultation for secession to become possible. The Government of Québec did not wish to turn a blind eye to the Government of Canada's intrusion into the judicial process. On second reading on 30 May 2000, it thus passed its own bill on the Exercise of the fundamental rights and prerogatives of the Québec people and the Québec State, in which section 13 stipulates that "No other parliament or government may reduce the powers, authority, sovereignty or legitimacy of the National Assembly, or impose constraint on the democratic will of the Québec people to determine its own future."

By making this stipulation, the Government of Québec in a sense endorsed the Reference that the Supreme Court of Canada rendered in August 1998, and which speaks of four general constitutional principles at the foundation of the Canadian federal pact. Those principles are federalism, democracy, the combination of rule of law and constitutionalism, and finally respect for minority rights. Indeed, most philosophers, political scientists and legal theorists have focused on these four principles in order to find an honourable, fully democratic solution to the Canadian constitutional crisis.[19]

From deep diversity to the multination

The Canadian context is very instructive with respect to first-degree diversity, namely the multiple origins of different Canadians. However, it is much less instructive when it comes to second-degree diversity, namely the cultural trajectories of the founding peoples. Second-degree diversity has rarely been taken into account by political leaders in Ottawa in their formulation of government policy, identification of cultural, social and political references, and engagement in constitutional reform. Like a republic that portrays itself as "one and indivisible", the Government of Canada seeks to impose its conditions on the federation's member states, thereby acting as if it was the only relevant player and as though it was able to freely impose its hegemony. This attitude had led all of Québec's political parties to take frequent action and propose major political changes to the operation of the Canadian federation in order to find solutions at the constitutional, economic and political levels.

The multination opens new avenues in the democratic discourse by legitimizing the claims of national communities in national states while enriching intercommunal life and democratizing political practices. Those who have been the primary proponents of the multination have strongly criticized the unitary national state. For example, Stéphane Pierré-Caps has noted that the national state is

> governed by the majority principle, in which relations between the state and the nation are organized in line with the "atomist–centralist" view according to which individuals are isolated and powerless in the face of the centralized state and its secular arm, the government. Moreover, the national state is completely identified with a bordered area of land, in which "might makes right" rules, namely the law of the majority of the population, the dominant national group. This is why political egality and freedom, which are asserted by classical majority democracy, can be achieved only in a multinational federation.[20]

Such domination often leads to grave injustice and suffering, and, specifically in the case of minority nations, situations that demand fair solutions to reduce the risk of ethno-cultural conflict and even break-up. The search for justice in order to achieve political stability has been one of the central objectives of the members of the Research Group on Multinational Societies since 1995.[21]

Analysts generally agree to distinguish two main federal traditions in Canada: territorial federalism and multinational federalism.[22] The former, which might more accurately be described as "mononational" federalism, is well-established in Canada outside Québec and consists in applying government policies in a uniform manner across the land, thereby implying that the country was built on the basis of a single political nation. This vision suggests that member states are interchangeable, including with respect to their historical obligations and the agreements that led to the initial constitutional arrangements.

This tradition's greatest breakthrough occurred when the Constitution was patriated in 1982, and the provinces of Canada and the central government together denied Québec's right to veto proposed constitutional amendments, though that right had been upheld in case law until then. The tradition's continuance helped to distance the Québécois and, it may be added, the First Nations, from Canadian institutions by depriving them of veritable sources of authenticity at the level of their primary spring of national identification. The main criticism of territorial federalism is that it sits uncomfortably with the federal principle[23] and treaty federalism.[24]

Among member states, Québec goes it alone in its opposition to Canadian territorial federalism. The political parties represented in the Québec National Assembly usually propose a binational vision of the country. The binational reading has received major support over the last 40 years: the Laurendeau–Dunton Commission (1963–1968) gave it some support at the federal level, and, in Québec, the Tremblay Commission (1953–1956), 1980 and 1995 referenda, and Bélanger–Campeau Commission on Québec's political and constitutional future (1990–1991) all called for respect for deep diversity, equality of the two founding peoples and Québec's predominant role in maintaining the French culture and language in the country.[25] Indeed, this view has raised the ire of English Canada, which fears producing unequal citizens by giving the Québécois privileges not available to other Canadians. This concern was clearly felt in the discussions surrounding the Meech Lake and Charlottetown Accords.[26]

The different traditions of federalism in Canada impact on the way political discussions and intercommunity relations are envisioned and interpreted. Yet, rather than seeking ways of bringing the two traditions closer together or developing a new modus operandi, the two schools tend to object to the admissibility of each other's point of view. This leads me to say that, in Canada, there is a mismatch between, on the one hand, the factual existence of several nations and, on the other hand, the standardizing model, which is relatively easily endorsed by all member states of the federation apart from Québec, that characterizes Ottawa's development and implementation of public policy.

The Québécois, who are generally opposed to territorial federalism, must reclaim the initiative and propose a multinational federalism able to accommodate First Nations' claims as well as their own.[27] Indeed, however the constitutional issue is resolved, it is already the case that Québec must deal with 11 internal nations.

In his discussion of national minorities in Europe, Stéphane Pierré-Caps suggests distinguishing between the political unity of the state and national unity.[28] This distinction is very important. Political unity is important, even essential, in that it enables various national communities to share a common future. National unity seeks to silence opposition groups or, at the very least, to make their life very difficult.[29] Perhaps because there are two very distinct traditions of federalism in Canada, the concepts that I employ are a little different from those of Pierré-Caps in that they are designed to describe differentiated federal citizenship rather than a standardized citizenship.

The Québécois, for example, are more likely to discuss self-government and non-subordination of powers, while Canadians outside Québec talk about pooling political resources and suggest standard models of governance. These concepts, based, as we have seen, on two different traditions, are equally valid and respectable. However, the implementation of each calls into question the legitimacy of the political actors and leads to frequent strife between the Québec national minority and the English-Canadian majority.

Trudeau versus Taylor

In modern times, the concepts of nation and nationalism have lost none of their relevance, quite the contrary. The notions of the multination and multinationalism[30] seem now to be among the ideas invoked as responses to nationality-based claims, though opposition, and even hostility, to them is palpable in both the political and academic arenas.[31]

Philip Resnick reminds us that

> As long as we operate under the assumption, as a majority of English Canadians does, that there is a single Canadian nation formed in 1867 of which Québécois and aboriginal peoples are a constituent part, there is relatively little room for discussion.[32]

In order to counter this trend, a number of Canadian and Québécois theorists have sought to re-imagine Canada's institutions in the form of a multinational federation, with a particular eye to rendering the Canadian government more legitimate in the eyes of First Nations and Québécois, and to allowing those nations to self-govern themselves.[33]

In this debate, which is central to Canadian political life, Trudeau and Taylor have advanced different and opposing visions.[34] Of the two, Pierre Trudeau has certainly left the greater mark on political life in Canada, as he was the inspiration for a whole generation of young Canadians. But many Québécois, a large proportion of members of First Nations, and proponents of provincial rights all took exception to his initiatives. For his part, Charles Taylor is certainly the philosopher who is best known in Canada and abroad for proposing communitarian liberalism as a solution to the problem of the denial of recognition for minority nations in existing states.

From Trudeau's point of view, the notion of dignity is related less to relations amongst individuals and groups than to a dialogue between individuals. Trudeau's moral theory is individualistic, which means that his understanding of freedom and human dignity is not influenced by collective values and projects. More specifically, Trudeau

> rejects the collectivist (and, he would say, reactionary) idea that values, traditions, and languages deserve respect and protection as a matter of right and justice. Too much cultural protectionism, he argues, inevitably shades into intolerance and finally a totalitarian denial of personal freedom in the name of group identity.[35]

Trudeau was famous for holding clear-cut positions, and he was little inclined towards intercultural reconciliation. He took his legitimacy from electoral results, and when he succeeded in obtaining a strong mandate, no matter what the support of the principal political communities, he implemented his government policies with little concern for their social and political repercussions.

Trudeau's inflexible attitude led to major discord in June 1969, when the White Paper on Indian policy was published (and subsequently withdrawn in the face of loud protests) and in 1982, when the Constitution was unilaterally patriated from Great Britain without the consent of the Québec National Assembly. In both cases, the political leaders who eventually took over from Trudeau were forced to promote plans for accommodation in order to better respond to the claims of those two national communities.

For example, consider the case of Brian Mulroney, Prime Minister of Canada from 1983 to 1993, who launched two major constitutional initiatives, namely, the draft Meech Lake Accord in 1987–1990 and the Charlottetown Accord in 1992. Both initiatives failed, which led the Government of Québec to hold a second referendum in 15 years on its future in the Canadian federation. With respect to the First Nations, there has certainly been some progress at the institutional level, for example, the 1999 creation of Nunavut and the *Delgamuukw* decision.[36] However, over ten years on, the primary recommendations of the Report of the Erasmus–Dussault Commission (1993–1996) are far from having been implemented.[37]

In contrast with Trudeau, Taylor argues that the notion of human dignity is inseparable from that of community-based identity. Moreover, according to Taylor, membership in a nation is the expression of a real, even emancipating, quest for authenticity and is the expression of a community feeling that makes it possible to counter the rampant atomism threatening contemporary life.[38] Throughout his academic career, Taylor has sought to advance new means of accommodating communities seeking affirmation, freedom and dignity. Ahead of his time, Taylor identified the problems inherent to the operation of states in which there is majority nationalism, and imagined humane, fair avenues for reconciliation. Today we can appreciate the accuracy of his analysis and the urgent need to demonstrate greater openness towards minority nations within states if we hope to avoid conflicts between peoples, such as those that have arisen in Czechoslovakia, Georgia, Lebanon, Cyprus and Iraq.[39]

Trudeau transformed the meaning of what it is to "be Canadian" in significant, possibly long-lasting ways. In a sense, and paradoxically, he bolstered Canadian nationalism by opposing the nationalist claims of Québécois and Aboriginal peoples. He presented his vision to Canadians as a zero-sum game in which people had to choose an identity and establish a hierarchy of their memberships. While he denounced nationalism, Trudeau was nevertheless himself a formidable nationalist. In *Federalism and the French Canadians*, he wrote,

> One way of offsetting the appeal of separatism is by investing tremendous amounts of time, energy, and money in nationalism *at the federal level*. [...] Resources must be diverted into such things as national flags, anthems, education, arts councils, broadcasting corporations, film boards.[40]

The ideas of both Trudeau and Taylor have had an impact on liberal societies, and have led decision-makers, intellectuals and the general public to adopt positions that align them with one or the other. While very influential with philosophers and theorists studying diversity, Taylor and communitarian philosophers have not managed to build a bulwark against the advances of procedural liberalism and territorial federalism. The entrenchment of the Canadian Charter of Rights and Freedoms in 1982 was territorial federalism's greatest advance in this sense.[41]

While, in many ways, it was a political advance, the Charter nonetheless poses problems with respect to pluralism in law. According to political scientist Alan C. Cairns, the Charter produces "a roving normative Canadianism oblivious to provincial boundaries [...] a homogenizing Charter-derived rights-bearing Canadianism".[42] The Charter's inclusion in the Constitution of Canada is thus part of a broad plan to construct nationality. In a way, it is the embodiment of a national policy to establish a single legal and political identity in Canada.[43]

James Tully notes that

> Yet, as Québec, the First Nations, and the provinces have sought to point out since 1982, the Charter fails to recognize and respect these ancient and complex federal relations [...]. The Charter seems to them to be a kind of voice over all the other passengers; as if it sought to lay down its vocabulary as canonical for the whole conversation, rather than seeing itself as one new voice in a federation of many voices with their own form of expression.[44]

Tully, who is a specialist in British constitutionalism, deplores the fact that the Québécois have not yet consented to the entrenchment of the Charter of Rights, a state of affairs that violates

> the oldest principle of federalism, and one of the oldest principles of western law, the principle on which the justice of our political institutions rests. *Quod omnes tangit ab omnibus tractari et approbari debet* – "what touches all must be approved by all".[45]

The struggle between political ideas inspired by Trudeau and the philosophical principles of Taylor has consequences for the way national groups in today's states co-exist. In Canada, many people are under the impression that Pierre Trudeau was correct. However, on the international scene, countries dealing with major political and constitutional crises do not hesitate to look to communitarian principles for solutions to problems involving representation and the fair division of power. In the next section we will see how this has given rise to a school of thought based on diversity but in which goals are not always shared.

The painful birth of a new Canadian school of diversity

Canada usually projects an idyllic image of itself onto the international scene. Politicians in Ottawa often hold the country up as a model that should be exported to the four corners of the Earth. The image of success, which is no longer debated but taken for granted, portrays Canada as a completed, flawless model. To use John Holmes' expression, it is painted as an "immaculate nation".[46] This portrait of Canada as a "perfect country" is constantly invoked abroad, but does not improve understanding of the reality that is actually at stake.

But which country, precisely, is it that is being invoked here? Is it that of Trudeau or of Taylor? It seems to me that the world is more in need of recognition than individual affirmation. The conflicts in Kurdistan, the Basque country, Kosovo, Ivory Coast, South Africa, Sri Lanka, Taiwan, Tibet and, closer to home, the suburbs of France require recognition of deep diversity, not the atomization of the population.

In Canada, there is a large body of literature on accommodating inter-community relations. This literature, including the works of Taylor, Will Kymlicka, James Tully, Margaret Moore, John McGarry, Kenneth McRoberts, Michel Seymour and members of the Research Group on Multinational Societies, has been translated into many languages around the world.[47] At the heart of these writings, we find the principles of justice, equality, reciprocity, historical continuity and deep diversity.[48] Respect for these principles will provide political regimes with the stability and social cohesion sought in states that encompass more than one national minority.

More recently, authors who used to share Pierre Trudeau's universalist ideas have distanced themselves from their earlier positions and joined the communitarians. For example, in *The Rights Revolution*, Michael Ignatieff suggests that we should avoid "majoritarianism" because "[r]eciprocity rather than strict symmetry for all is the way to move beyond a politics of concession and threat into a process of mutual recognition, in which each side acknowledges the distinctiveness of the other".[49]

The authors belonging to the Canadian school of diversity do not go unopposed. Their analyses have produced many unfavourable reactions. For example, in his works on Aboriginal peoples, such as *First Nations? Second Thoughts*,[50] Tom Flanagan sees no point in taking Aboriginal claims into account in building Canada. Instead, Flanagan suggests implementing policies of cultural assimilation and homogenization in favour of the dominant culture. Because it takes the side of majority Canadian nationalism, his proposal leads to irreconcilable differences between Aboriginal and non-Aboriginal peoples. Other authors, such as Alan Cairns,[51] distance themselves from Flanagan's position and suggest government policies that are more conciliatory and sensitive to differences. However, they find it impossible to follow through with their reasoning, which would entail proposing a multinational system in Canada. Indeed, Cairns' primary concern is the obligation to identify with the (Canadian) whole and to show primary allegiance to its central institutions. Thus, Cairns' view does not resolve the problem of recognition for national communities in the state (though this is often obscured by political players), but it is certainly a significant improvement over Flanagan's position.

The ties that unite Canadians outside Québec, Aboriginal people and the Québécois must be conceived in a new framework that takes into account mutual recognition, reciprocity, continuity of legal traditions, maintenance of multiple conversations and the parties' free consent to arrive at renewed accords. Thus, as Tully reminds us, it is precisely these relations, with their "time-honoured traditions and conventions, which historically constitute this strange multiplicity and preserve the cultural, legal, and political diversity of [the Canadian federation's] members".[52]

This chapter ends with a warning. There is a great temptation today for proponents of procedural rights (who often frame their claims in terms of the equality principle) to clothe their discourse in the language of multinationality, which disguises what is really at stake. We should note in passing two works published in 2005: *In Defence of Multinational Citizenship*[53] and *Multicultural Nationalism: Civilizing Difference, Constituting Community*.[54] The former is a defence of the state cloaked in the recognition of deep diversity and the privileging of majority nationalism. The latter is an account of political debates in Canada outside Québec that pays little attention to debates in Québec and within Aboriginal nations.

In *Multicultural Nationalism*, Kernerman celebrates the fact that there is one Canadian school of thought based on equality and another inspired by the right to difference. He seeks a dialogue that is essentially limited to a discussion among English-speaking Canadians and pays little attention to the other national communities that make Canada a multinational federation. In short, the goal of both works is simple, even simplistic: *unity for the sake of unity*.

Like the American thinkers who sought to position themselves in relation to the English tradition, many "Canadian" thinkers have sought to achieve a synthesis of those two great traditions. On one hand, they have retained from English authors the desire for unity based on deep diversity, and, on the other hand, they have tried to adopt the American principle of identity-based differentiation aimed at individual emancipation. As we have seen, these approaches face serious challenges, especially when founding nations have to be recognized in existing states.

The Canadian myth of a national state that has succeeded in recognizing first-degree diversity is strong, but the frequent resistance from Aboriginal nations and the sovereigntist threat to hold a third referendum to obtain full recognition reveal serious tensions in the Canadian federation.

It is difficult to imagine an honourable end to the Canadian question unless the focus of the discussion returns to the treaty federalism proposed by the First Nations and the multinational federalism advanced by deep diversity thinkers in Canada and Québec. In conclusion, we have to wonder whether the goals of standardization and homogenization are not obsolete. The Belgian, British and Swiss examples merit greater study so that the ties uniting Canadians do not deprive national founding communities of their freedom.[55]

4 Executive federalism and the exercise of democracy in Canada[1]

Political players often lack the commitment to respect the basic principles underlying federalism itself. Today, a democratic theory of federalism is needed. Catalalan and Québec researchers are perhaps those who have done the most in recent years to develop such a theory; for example, the researchers whom we mentioned above, such as Enric Fossas, Montserrat Guibernau and Ferran Requejo, who have focused on multinational Spain and the members of the Research Group on Multinational Societies,[2] who study Canada as a multination.

Two avenues of solution will be examined in the chapters that complete this book. In the present chapter, we will explore the intrinsic values of executive federalism as an approach to managing conflict in contemporary liberal states in which there is deep national diversity. This approach could be described as minimalist, and might lead to a first-degree multinational system. In the next chapter, we will study the multination in greater detail as a promising avenue for bringing national communities together on the basis of second-degree representation in state institutions. The latter approach, which we describe as maximalist, seems more promising for the historical nations in Spain, the First Nations and Québec in Canada, the Scottish and Welsh nations in the United Kingdom, and Flanders and Wallonia in the new composite country of Belgium.

This chapter is structured around three points. First, we review the notion of executive federalism and its utility in managing political conflicts. Second, we assess the greatest challenges facing executive federalism at a time when states are gradually coming to terms with globalization.[3] Third, we examine the counter-hegemonic potential of executive federalism for minority nations. This is relevant as many contemporary states seek to adopt increasingly centralized institutions on the grounds that they are needed to meet the challenge of globalization, but at the same time silently develop monist national projects and depreciate the worth of national diversity as a public good that provides people with diverse, authentic contexts in which they can make choices.

Although executive federalism could certainly undergo significant democratic refinements, I do not feel that it constitutes a serious threat to democracy. On the contrary, it deepens our understanding of democracy. More significantly and disturbingly, it is the emergence of monistic identity policies in a number of contemporary states, particularly Canada, that confirms that in some cases political leaders flagrantly disregard the social and cultural foundations of the polity. This requires immediate, sustained attention because it undermines political actors' trust in their own institutions and shakes the foundations that are meant to unite the polity and give it relevance.

Conceptual considerations and historical developments

Students of federalism have employed an impressive number of definitions to describe the Canadian variation. Many adjectives have been utilized to portray the types of interactions that take place between executive bodies in the intergovernmental realm. Whether Canadian federalism is described as colonial, imperial, classical, administrative, cooperative, collaborative, constitutional or competitive,[4] it remains that the major players who manage the federation have virtually always come from the executive branches of the various governments. The epithets all reflect distinct types of federalism from different periods. For example, Richard Simeon and Ian Robinson show that executive federalism gradually replaced administrative federalism in the 1950s and 1960s as public servants were pressed to find relevant answers to growing western provincialism, Québec nationalism, and regional and class inequalities. As a result, Canada experienced a burst of state expansion in that generally affluent period. The challenges politicized intergovernmental relations and led to wrangling between the member states of the federation and the central government, suggesting that the BNA Act was showing its age. Simeon and Robinson argue that, in the 1960s,

> the perceived need for constitutional change meant that federal–provincial relations became an intensely political, as opposed to a largely technical and bureaucratic, process. Federalism had to adapt to these new demands and, in so doing, the era of executive federalism was born.[5]

I agree with Simeon and Robinson that Canadian federalism has evolved considerably over the years, but feel that it is a mistake to oppose administrative and executive federalism as they do. Administrative federalism is simply another form of executive federalism, and the same can be said about the categories of colonial, imperial, classical, administrative, cooperative, constitutional, collaborative and competitive federalism that have been employed to depict federal–provincial relations. These are simply variants of executive federalism, not institutionally distinct models that embody shifts in the fundamental features of Canadian federalism. In other words, executive federalism is a permanent feature of Canadian politics. Governance of the Canadian federation has always been through the executive institutions of federalism.

The establishment of the Canadian federation in 1867 was achieved without popular involvement; it was the result of elite accommodation rather than of a desire to overthrow a political regime. Reg Whitaker has remarked that in sharp contrast to the drafting of the American, French and German constitutions, the BNA Act of 1867, Canada's founding document, is "almost entirely innocent of any recognition of the people as the object of the constitutional exercise" and constitutes "an arrangement between elites, particularly between political elites".[6] This demarcates the Canadian version of federalism from the American-style people's constitution, as Peter Russell has noted.[7] This elite-driven vision of federalism has clearly influenced the way Canadians have imagined the relationships at the origin of the pact and how they have tried to pursue them since.

Until the Second World War, the two orders of government operated in relative isolation. Aside from during the Great Depression of the 1930s, there was little need to consult and establish joint priorities. A classical version of federalism based on a watertight approach to jurisdictions had taken hold in Canada. However, when cooperation was necessary, such as in areas of shared jurisdiction like immigration and agriculture, executive branches met to address potential conflicts. An example of this is the first intergovernmental conference in 1868.[8]

During the first decades of Confederation, the central government tended to pursue a nation-building strategy best illustrated by implementation of the National Policy of 1879, of which the three pillars were immigration, the construction of a railroad and a tariff policy that guaranteed merchants a captive market. This was compounded by the inherited imperial statute and a colonial political culture.

Throughout the twentieth century, Great Britain's powers (for example, the power to appoint lieutenant governors and the Governor General, to resolve disputes between members of the federation, and to determine foreign policy) were devolved to the central government.[9] This made provinces second-class partners. Formal powers of disallowance and reservation also bolstered the weight of the central government.[10]

Only nine First Ministers' Conferences were held before the Depression in the 1930s and "almost all of those held before World War I were interprovincial conferences with no significant federal participation".[11] Although this period saw little in the way of federal–provincial relations, the central government's non-participation was a conscious decision on the part of the Executive, and strengthened interprovincial relations. The "watertight compartments" model of federalism began to be questioned more frequently during the first two decades of the twentieth century, and the model was said to be incapable of dealing with the crisis triggered by the Great Depression of the 1930s.[12] From then on, contact between the central government and the provinces became more frequent and formalized.[13] Executive federalism was becoming more apparent.

With the development of the welfare state, the situation started to evolve more quickly as public servants began exchanging more and more information. The ensuing period witnessed the rise of modern bureaucracy in Canada and the expansion of governments' regulatory functions. The focus turned to areas of policy such as telecommunications, transportation, energy, natural resources development, and consumer and environmental protection, which generally cut across provincial and federal jurisdictions.[14] Governments were becoming interdependent.

Moreover, development of the welfare state required greater involvement from the provinces since health, education and transportation, all of which are under exclusive provincial jurisdiction, are crucial to economic-development strategy. There was a need to better define the roles and responsibilities of every level of government as the bureaucracy expanded. By the early 1970s, the machinery of executive federalism was well in place, and specialized departments for managing intergovernmental relations had been set up to attend to the needs of the central government and the member states of the Canadian federation. First Ministers' Conferences were becoming a major tool in the management of federal–provincial relations.

Donald Smiley was one of the first political scientists to make use of the concept of executive federalism. According to Smiley, it refers to "the relations between elected and appointed officials of the two orders of government in federal–provincial interactions and among the executives of the provinces in interprovincial interactions".[15] The decision-making process primarily involves cabinet members and senior bureaucrats in programme and public-policy establishment. In the course of related discussions, key issues of governance are raised since the executives are accountable to their electorates through their legislatures. Stephan Dupré later refined this definition by removing interprovincialism from the definition. According to Dupré, these relations should be depicted as expressions of "executive interprovincialism" because they are more often than not responses to executive federalism. Thus, executive federalism refers to intergovernmental relations that involve the two orders of government with a view to enabling federal and provincial executives (first ministers, cabinet ministers and appointed officials) to control their respective political arenas.

Today, executive federalism is an institution that is familiar to all observers of Canadian politics. It has also been a key feature in the development of a series of constitutional proposals and economic arrangements, including the patriation of the Canadian Constitution from Great Britain in 1982, the Meech Lake Accord (1987–1990), the Charlottetown Accord (1992) and the Agreement on Internal Trade (1994). In addition to providing a framework for negotiations between federal and provincial government officials, executive federalism has played a leading role in many other circumstances. Ronald Watts has described the process aptly:

> The importance of this pattern of executive federalism has stemmed not only from the frequency with which first ministers, ministers and senior officials have interacted, but also from the critical role that this interaction has played: first, in the range of programs and services provided by Canadian governments to their citizens, second, in the discussion of economic policy including trade relations with the United States, and third, in the revision of the Constitution itself, most notably in the period leading up to the Constitution Act, 1982, and again in producing the Constitutional Accord of 1987.[16]

More recently, we have seen executive federalism at work in Canada with the implementation of the Social Union Framework Agreement (1999), the Health Accord (2004) and the Accord on Equalization (2004). First ministers, cabinet ministers and senior officials of the two orders of government meet frequently to iron out differences. According to Marc-Antoine Adam, in 2003 as many as 117 meetings involving these different authorities took place,[17] confirming that executive federalism continues to be a key institution in the management of the Canadian federation.

Executive federalism is an institution that has had equal numbers of supporters and detractors in Canada. The way its merits are weighed varies considerably between English-speaking and French-speaking political scientists, but also within the two linguistic groups. Executive federalism is associated[18] with many achievements, including greater mobility for people between Canadian provinces, improvements to the healthcare system, the establishment of two pension plans (one in Québec and the other applying to the rest of Canada), improved federal–provincial relations and the fight against regional disparities. From a Québécois point of view, executive federalism has helped to reduce tensions between Québec City and Ottawa. For example, under Prime Minister Lester B. Pearson, it became possible to withdraw from certain federal programmes and to receive financial compensation. Executive federalism also made it possible for Québec to play a major role in immigration under the governments of Pierre Elliott Trudeau and Brian Mulroney. Note that the latter demonstrated greater openness than his predecessor by according Québec the status of participating government in the Francophonie.

Over the years, executive federalism in the decision-making process has also led to considerable tension between the orders of government, each of which is eager to maintain its entire jurisdiction.[19] Each party seeks credit for its actions and tries to depreciate the real participation of the other order of government in the implementation of various measures. Over time, two visions of power sharing have taken form in Canada: one favours central government domination of the federation's member states, while the other encourages the provinces' leadership.[20]

Twenty-five years ago, Donald Smiley, a renowned specialist of Canadian federalism, delivered a strong attack against executive federalism, and his criticism is still relevant today. Smiley identified six primary defects of executive federalism. It:

1   leads to undue secrecy in the management of public affairs.
2   produces a very low level of citizen involvement in the decision-making process.
3   renders public servants relatively unaccountable to legislatures and the general public.

4   creates obstacles to public examination of government policies.
5   increases governmental interventions.
6   creates conflicts between orders of government that concern only
    the interests of politicians and bureaucrats.[21]

Smiley's criticism came at a time when executive federalism was
generally defended by other Canadian specialists in the field. Smiley
added his voice to that of left-leaning intellectuals, who considered
that executive federalism did not do enough for workers and people
in general. John Porter's work, which was done in the 1960s but
brought back into the limelight in the 1970s and 1980s by a number
of Canadian specialists of political economy, was highly critical of
executive federalism. He inspired the most progressive segments of
Canadian society to oppose it, and claimed

> federalism ... has meaning only for politicians and senior civil
> servants who work with the complex machinery that they have
> set up, as well as for the scholars who provide a continuing com-
> mentary on it, but that it has very little meaning for the bulk of
> the population.[22]

Porter went so far as to suggest that, in Canada, provincial autonomy
was equivalent to "federal usurpation",[23] thus providing ammunition
for adversaries of classical federalism. This strengthened the opposition of those who believed that discussions concerning the division of
powers are a waste of time and energy.

The principal challenges facing executive federalism

Emergence of a system

What accounts for Canada's strong tradition of executive federalism?
In a 2004 book entitled *Federalism*, Jennifer Smith provides four
reasons that are worth highlighting. First, for Smith, "the provinces
are much stronger players in the system than those who framed the
Constitution ever anticipated".[24] Their strength derives from the fact
that the prominence of the jurisdictions for which they are accountable, namely, healthcare, education and transportation, has grown significantly over the years. Their responsibilities in these fields lead the
provinces to negotiate with the central government for more tax
dollars since Ottawa has ampler access to tax revenues. Second,
even though there is a second house that could play a central role in

representing the provinces in Ottawa, the Senate's function has been limited to one of "sober second thought about legislative proposals sent to it by the House of Commons".[25] As a result, according to Smith,

> no body within the federal government is designed to represent the provinces or speak for them in federal councils, which leaves the provincial governments as the singular agents of provincial concerns, not just in the provincial capitals but at the federal level as well.[26]

In other words, intra-state federalism in the Canadian context has never been very successful, and this in turn has favoured interstate federalism.

The third reason identified by Smith suggests that the Canadian parliamentary system contains the seeds of interstate federalism. It is well-known that in parliamentary systems the executive branch is dominant. "The engine of the system is the political executive, meaning the prime minister (or premier) and the cabinet, who together almost always dominate the legislature."[27] The nature of the Canadian party system, stressing party discipline, contributes to buffer the governing party from serious challenges emanating from the legislature as its leader knows that s/he can count on its members' support when there is a majority government. As such, interstate federalism cannot be considered the most democratic feature of the system, considering that it allows the executive to escape its obligation to be accountable to the legislature.

To these institutional factors, Smith adds a cultural explanation for the strength of executive federalism in Canada. In essence, established rules, conventions and traditions have always resulted from "the dominance of governmental elites in decision making, and public deference to the results".[28] Admittedly, there have been some direct appeals to Canadians over the years, for example, with regards to Conscription in the First and Second World Wars, and the Meech Lake and Charlottetown Accords (since the provincial elections in New Brunswick and Manitoba put the issues to the voters), but Canadians still seem inclined to delegate authority.

Smith's assessment of the strength and persistence of executive federalism in Canada is compelling. However, it can account neither for the highs and lows experienced by executive federalism over the years, nor for its rebound following the Second World War.

A fifth aspect, namely that of government requirements, has to be taken into account to explain why executive federalism has been strengthened. The emergence and consolidation of the welfare state in Canada has meant that governments can no longer work in isolation from one another. Government policies, at one level or another, have come to affect the objectives of other orders of government. As the central government has expanded its activities in various policy fields, clashes have become more frequent, especially between the governments in Ottawa and Québec City.

The Government of Québec has always assumed special responsibility towards the francophone population in Canada, and has demanded financial assistance and powers to provide its citizens with opportunities equal to those of Canadians outside Québec. Over the years, the Québec government has sought new funding and additional powers and staunchly opposed federal encroachments as it has built a modern welfare state of its own. The last half-century in Canadian politics has seen politicization of the division of powers, which has led to several conflicts between prime ministers and premiers, with the former seeking to build an integrated and at times homogeneous Canada, and the latter believing in a diverse country in which each province provides a distinct context of choice for its inhabitants.

Executive federalism emerged long before the era of government interdependence. It was present at the time of Confederation and will be with us for the foreseeable future. Executive federalism has assisted political elites in managing contentious issues. It is indeed hard to imagine that executive federalism might vanish one day, when we consider

1 the presence of strong, autonomous provinces that are in charge of major policy sectors;
2 a Westminster-style parliamentary system;
3 a party system that is essentially confederal in nature and stresses party discipline;
4 a political culture that has tended to welcome a top–down approach to politics; and
5 strong interdependence among governments, which requires interaction.

Executive federalism under stress

Until the 1970s, political stakeholders did not see executive federalism as controversial. In political circles and the population at large, the principles of elite accommodation were widely accepted.[29] The Canadian federal union was considered to be the affair of political elites coming together as brokers without the direct involvement of the people in management of the state. This was viewed as a legitimate process and a practice to be advocated.

Following the election of the Parti Québécois (PQ) in November 1976, this approach to Canadian politics began to be challenged. Inspired by high democratic standards, PQ leader René Lévesque promised to hold a referendum on sovereignty-association if successful in the 1976 provincial election. Lévesque later lived up to his promise by holding a referendum on 20 May 1980. As Alain Noël has pointed out, "for the first time in Canadian history, the people were considered sovereign in constitutional matters".[30] We were moving from elite accommodation to a new era in which citizen involvement would be the norm.

Immediately following the defeat of the Québec nationalists in the 1980 referendum, Pierre Elliott Trudeau, Canada's Prime Minister at the time, initiated the process of patriating the Canadian constitution from Great Britain. The Trudeau Liberals took advantage of the nationalist defeat to go forward with patriation, adding a complex amending formula and entrenching a Charter of Rights and Freedoms. In the process, disagreements among the member states of the federation as well as between those states and the central government were arising as never before. Initially, a common front of eight provinces opposed the central government's plan to patriate unless an agreement was reached with respect to power-sharing and an amending formula, and limitations were set on federal spending power.

Québec played a key role in the process that led to a coalition of eight provinces, known as the "Gang of Eight", that agreed to hold a firm shared position. In the meantime, the central government launched its own "endeavour to legitimize its proposals after a stalemate with the provinces arose".[31] The objective was clear, namely to use the "people" and special interests to give the central government leverage in negotiations with the provinces. This strategy proved popular with Canadians because it gave citizens and special interests more prominence in the political arena at a time when rights consciousness was on the rise.

When negotiations between the provinces and the central government reached an impasse on 4 November 1981, Pierre Trudeau suggested to the premiers the possibility of holding a pan-Canadian referendum. This strategy was intended to isolate the Québec Premier and thus break the common front. When his plan seemed to be in trouble at the negotiating table, Trudeau mused:

> How do we resolve this [stalemate]. Maybe we should agree to keep talking and hold a referendum in two years' time? There, that's a new offer. [...] Surely a great democrat like yourself [Lévesque] won't be against a referendum?[32]

As expected, Lévesque agreed with Trudeau's suggestion. This was interpreted by the other members of the Gang of Eight as a Québec defection since they were opposed to such a scenario. The provincial coalition collapsed, and the rest is history. The proposed Canadian referendum never took place, all the premiers with the exception of Lévesque agreed to the central government's package deal, and patriation occurred shortly thereafter.[33] The fact that negotiations between federal and provincial leaders took place behind closed doors irritated citizens and groups, amongst them Aboriginal leaders, who felt that such a lack of transparency undermined the democratic process. However, this did not prevent Ottawa from proceeding with patriation. The central government undermined executive federalism as a political resource by addressing Canadians directly instead of inviting provincial leaders to act as go-betweens.

During this intense period of constitutional negotiation in Canada, political elites played Russian roulette with established federal practices. The conventional rules that fortified executive federalism were bent frequently. This process increased Québec's isolation in the game of federal–provincial politics. It opened a breach separating Québec from the other provinces, and this had major repercussions for Québec during the Meech Lake (1987–1990) and Charlottetown (1992) constitutional negotiations.

With a view to correcting the exclusion of Québec in 1982 at the time of patriation, Prime Minister Brian Mulroney launched a programme to bring Québec back into the constitutional family with "honour and enthusiasm". This led to the signing of the Meech Lake Accord in 1987 by all of the first ministers of Canada, which reconnected with the convention of executive federalism in intergovernmental matters. Political leaders acted as representatives of the people, as they had always done in constitutional matters. However, as is clear from the immediate aftermath of the failed accord, the leaders had underestimated the force of the Charter culture that had taken hold since 1982.[34] What emerged was a growing feeling that citizens' groups and socio-cultural, non-territorial actors had the right to be heard in the process, and that the "people" could no longer be taken for granted when political leaders wanted to reach constitutional arrangements. Alan C. Cairns is surely the one who has best encapsulated the implications of the 1982 patriation for constitutional politics in Canada, and its lasting impact on executive federalism:

> The Charter brought new groups into the constitutional order or, as in the case of aboriginals, enhanced a pre-existing constitutional status. It bypassed governments and spoke directly to Canadians by defining them as bearers of rights, as well as by according specific constitutional recognition to women, aboriginals, official-language minority populations, ethnic groups through the vehicle of multiculturalism, and to those social categories explicitly listed in the equality rights section of the Charter. The Charter thus reduced the relative status of governments and strengthened that of the citizens who received constitutional encouragement to think of themselves as constitutional actors.[35]

The politicians who had succeeded in patriating the Constitution Act 1982 continued to undermine the image of executive federalism as a democratic tool in federal–provincial negotiations. A process that had been viewed as legitimate less than a decade earlier and that had profoundly changed the way Canada governed itself, was increasingly discredited. To stress the point made by Richard Simeon and David Cameron with respect to the 1982 patriation:

> what right, what mandate, did eleven "men in suits" meeting behind closed doors have to make fundamental changes in Canada's Constitution? In a new era of participatory politics, Charter-based rights discourse, and citizen distrust of elites of all kinds, the basic legitimacy of the Canadian pattern of intergovernmental relations was called into question.[36]

The role of governments as special constitutional players was reduced as they were surrounded by an overabundance of voices that deemed themselves legitimate actors in the decision-making process.[37] This provocative image of white "men in suits" was used several times to denounce the elitist nature of the process by politicians who were opposed to revisiting the exclusion of Québec from the Constitutional deal using the constitutional formula that had been employed until then.

During the Charlottetown negotiations, the Mulroney government made a genuine effort to engage the population at large by holding a series of town hall meetings and public conferences with a view to finding a constitutional means of extricating Canada from the political crisis into which it had blundered. In October 1992, it all culminated in a referendum in Québec, and another in Canada outside of Québec, on what should be done to achieve constitutional peace. The constitutional changes considered led to a new practice emphasizing the obligation to consult "the people" directly.[38] As Kathy Brock reminds us with respect to the Charlottetown Accord:

> Negotiations between governments were preceded by the most extensive round of public consultations on the constitution ever held in Canada. [...] Although negotiations were conducted in private between elected and appointed government officials, the process appeared more deliberate and open. [...] The talks were more inclusive and representative, involving representatives from the federal, provincial, and territorial governments and the four major national Aboriginal organizations. Women's organizations were consulted during the talks as well.[39]

This new constitutional round was meant to correct some of the undemocratic, unrepresentative, elitist and secretive features that were said to exist at the time of the negotiations that led to the patriation of the Constitution in 1982 and to the Meech Lake proposals in 1987. The idea that was gaining prominence was that governments required a substantial popular majority before making any changes to the Constitution. If Meech Lake failed due to insufficient popular support, Charlottetown went down due to an excess of consultative process as there was an attempt to pull in both governmental and societal interests.[40] With the introduction of societal interests at large, the difficulty of reaching a decision had increased ten-fold.

The period stretching from Meech Lake to Charlottetown was particularly difficult for proponents of executive federalism in Canada. Not only were the spokespersons of social groups on the defensive because they felt that any move to reconcile with Québec was a threat to recently achieved gains, but the federal Liberals had abandoned executive federalism altogether, and were taking advantage of the political goodwill they had won in the eyes of the new, recently mobilized groups to further impose their domineering vision of federalism.

With the election of the federal Liberals under Jean Chrétien in 1993, constitutional changes by constitutional means were discontinued. Even though their predecessors had failed to bring Québec back into the constitutional family, the federal Liberals reverted to a phase of "politics as usual", stressing job creation and good government. According to Harvey Lazar, the new strategy was aimed at "dealing with issues, one at a time, employing legislative or administrative solutions, on the basis of the concrete circumstances of each file".[41] A certain form of executive federalism, based on an ad-hoc strategy, was resurrected, and citizens as well as societal groups were kept at bay for the time being as the central government attempted to impose indivisible political leadership. Constitutional issues were presented from a technical angle rather than as fundamental questions concerning community relations.

The Social Union Framework Agreement provides the best illustration of the emerging trend of implementing a centralizing vision through non-constitutional means.[42] Following major unexpected cuts in federal transfers to the provinces in the 1995 federal budget, provincial capacity to intervene was severely undermined.[43] The premiers expressed their frustration in a brief tabled in December 1995 by the Ministerial Council on Social Policy Reform and Renewal, in which they advocated management of the federal union "on a true partnership basis".[44] The Québec government added its voice to make the premiers' statement unanimous. At the end of the exchanges between the orders of government, the federal government completely revamped the premiers' proposal to substitute its own interpretation and impose its own conditions. Yet, in February 1999, all premiers, with the notable exception of Québec's, agreed to the new deal even though their claims had not been respected and the spirit of federalism had been betrayed.[45]

From 1995 to January 2006, "the role of the provinces seems to have been largely confined to saying 'yes' or 'no' to the amount [of money] and negotiating for enhanced flexibility on how it might be spent".[46] Ottawa continued to impose its own conditions on provincial governments and took a "take it or leave it" approach to intergovernmental relations. Such a domineering approach to federal–provincial relations certainly further alienated provinces from the central government, and contributed to the defeat of the federal Liberals on 23 January 2006 and their replacement by Stephen Harper's Conservatives, known for their favourable stance towards provincial rights.

In the meantime, provincial governments, under the leadership of Québec, created the Council of the Federation to counteract Ottawa's centralizing thrust under the Liberals. On 5 December 2003, provincial and territorial leaders signed the Founding Agreement with a view to open a new chapter in intergovernmental relations in Canada. It is too early to tell how successful this initiative will be, but we do know that the premiers have identified a series of shortcomings in Canadian federalism. As Marc-Antoine Adam notes, up to this point the focus has been "on the equal status of Canada's two orders of government, neither subordinate to the other, and on the need to respect the Constitution and the division of powers as well as the diversity within the federation".[47]

After a full decade of unilateral federalism under the Chrétien's Liberals (1993–2004) and a generally disappointing period under Paul Martin's Liberals, in which there was a failure to accommodate provincial demands, the federal elections held in January 2006 suggested the beginning of a new era in federal–provincial relations.

When majority nationalism trumps executive federalism

By all accounts, at a theoretical level, shortcomings associated with executive federalism in Canada have little to do with its perceived democratic deficiencies. The greatest problems of representation linked to a system of executive federalism arise in the special context of a single-nation conception of a country. Criticisms of executive federalism too often veil manifestations of majority nationalism, which is precisely what the institution of federalism is meant to preclude.

We have already examined some of the challenges posed to executive federalism during the patriation debates of 1981–1982. Most of the process involved federal–provincial actors at a time when executive federalism was considered a defining feature of Canadian federalism. It must be remembered that Trudeau threatened to call a referendum after negotiations between the provincial governments and Ottawa had reached an impasse. Trudeau denounced the institutions of executive federalism at the time, suggesting that they were unrepresentative of the general will of citizens and that there was an urgent need to eliminate a growing democratic deficit in Canada. Once he had his way, Trudeau did not call a referendum to settle the issue.

Trudeau was more interested in breaking the provincial governments' common front than in giving a voice to Canadians. Towards the end of the process, his strategy succeeded, and the coalition collapsed. Ironically, Pierre Trudeau, the very person who had challenged the legitimacy of executive federalism, accepted becoming the godfather of a constitutional accord reached at night behind closed doors between executive branches, and without any representation from Québec. This inevitably caused unprecedented friction with the Government of Québec.[48]

For Trudeau, only Ottawa could speak on behalf of all Canadians. He believed he was the only political leader who had a pan-Canadian mandate and could act as a true representative of the national interest of Canada. From his point of view, whether the system was federal or not, there could be only one *demos* and it would have been a grave constitutional error to admit that the provinces could present themselves as the spokespersons of other *demoi*.[49] This way of seeing things led to clashes between the member states of the federation and the central government because both orders are legitimate representatives and speak, at different levels, on behalf of their respective communities.

André Burelle, a former speech-writer and long-time advisor to Trudeau, summarized the emerging monistic vision of Canada that grew in popularity under Trudeau's federal Liberals beginning in the 1960s and that has never lost ground:

> This vision, promoted by Trudeau, Chrétien and company, is that of a civic "one-nation" Canada, subject to a "national" charter of rights and freedoms, allergic to the collective rights of the country's founding peoples, and served by a federal system that pits thirteen "junior" governments against one "senior" government responsible for ensuring that the "national" interest prevails over the parochialism of the provinces and territories. In this conception of Canada, "national sovereignty" belongs entirely to the "Canadian people" who give Ottawa the exclusive responsibility of ensuring the greater good of the nation and guaranteeing equal rights to citizens across the country.[50]

Trudeau and like-minded Canadian politicians believed that sovereignty cannot be shared and that orders of government amount to nothing more than lower levels of government over which the central level reigns supreme. Yet, it seems that this kind of interpretation runs counter to the national interest because it does not take into account the fact that, in a federal democracy, the central government is only one player among many others.[51] The central government simply cannot be viewed as the only and true representative of the country's national interest. In fact, federalism ought to be interpreted as a system of government that can produce different majorities on different scales with a view to constraining the power of the central government and guaranteeing minorities sovereignty in some areas of jurisdiction. As Reginald Whitaker says:

> Modern federalism is an institutionalization of the formal limitation of the national majority will as the legitimate ground for legislation. Any functioning federal system denies by its very processes that the national majority is the efficient expression of the sovereignty of the people: a federation replaces this majority with a more diffuse definition of sovereignty. It does this not by denying the democratic principle, as such, but by advancing a more complex definition of democratic citizenship. As a result, individuals find political expression and representation in dual (sometimes even multiple) manifestations which may even be contradictory and antagonistic.[52]

Trudeau's vision of the country contrasts sharply with that of Whitaker in that the latter advances a democratic theory about the well-being of federal states. In short, Trudeau and his followers fail to appreciate that the Canadian polity is composed of many different majorities and that it can be considered and incarnated just as legitimately on the basis of distinct territories.

This brings me to an important point made by Michael Burgess when discussing the links between federalism, nationalism and the national state:

> If the principal *raison d'être* of a federation is its continuing capacity to protect, promote, and preserve one or more sub-state nationalism, [...] then its primary purpose will be subject to persistent scrutiny. The federal government [...] will always be the object of what Acton might have called a "healthy scepticism".[53]

The point is that it is essential for minorities to be empowered so as to be able to act as majorities in the policy fields necessary for their own historical continuity.

Returning to our discussion of Meech Lake, it should be noted that executive federalism was challenged at that time by the fact that it did not reflect Canada's majority nationalism in a positive manner. Indeed, this phenomenon grew throughout the Trudeau and Chrétien years. In fact, executive federalism was challenged not so much with respect to democracy but for the simple reason that it projected a composite image of Canada. In order to shed some light on the changes to Canadian political culture in recent years, let us look at how two highly respected specialists in Canada interpret the Meech Lake failure.

On the one hand, Alan Cairns concludes that the Meech Lake Accord was perceived by "many citizens and groups outside of Quebec [...] as an undesired diminution of their sense of themselves as Canadians".[54] On the other hand, Peter Russell concludes that Meech Lake's failure

> demonstrated the populist appeal of the principle of "provincial equality" outside of Quebec. A policy of providing special arrangement for Quebec entails a political risk which federal leaders will be loathe to assume. We also learned through Meech how unacceptable a purely Quebec round of constitutional change is to the rest-of-Canada.[55]

The failures of the Meech Lake and Charlottetown constitutional accords in 1990 and 1992 illustrate the extent to which political leaders from Canada outside of Québec have departed from the very foundations of the federalism that is at the origin of the founding pact. Guy Laforest's work provides solid confirmation of this.[56]

More recently, the implementation of the Social Union Framework Agreement (SUFA) in 1999 and signing of the Agreement on Equalization in autumn 2004, with perhaps the exception of the Health Care Accord in September 2004, tend to confirm a vision of the country with a firmly centrist bias. It is ironic that the SUFA negotiations took place behind closed doors and that few condemned this. The repercussions were significant for federalism considering that the federal government's spending power is to be used in areas of exclusive provincial jurisdiction and new rules governing intergovernmental relations concerning social policy were forced on the provinces alone. What is even more disturbing from a Québec standpoint is that, even though it is not a signatory to the agreement, it must nevertheless comply with the SUFA. In the end, Canadian majority nationalism has simply prevailed over Canada's federal structure.

If Meech Lake was drawn up in a secretive manner and is unrepresentative of a wide range of opinions in Canada, what are we to make of SUFA? Despite opposition from all of Québec's political parties, SUFA was imposed and little effort was made to address Québec's legitimate concerns. Alain Noël considers that we

> cannot avoid noting that this preoccupation with process only emerged when the English-speaking majority overwhelmingly felt

dissatisfied with the outcome, and disappeared later on, when more palatable agreements were signed behind closed doors (the 1999 Social Union Framework Agreement is a case in point).[57]

In short, dissatisfaction with executive federalism arose only when it worked against majority nationalism, and was well received when it helped to consolidate the image of Canada sought by the English-Canadian majority.

Donald Smiley's critique of executive federalism shows that it does have flaws: a certain lack of transparency, a low level of citizen-involvement, loss of some legislative prerogative, less public scrutiny, encouragement of government spending and possibly greater conflict between orders of government. Such criticisms should not be brushed aside. They have to be taken into account in improvements to the operation of a federal system based on executive federalism. However, there are also very valid reasons to support true executive federalism.

From a Québec perspective, the main issue at stake in the institution of executive federalism is the frequency with which the central government has bent the rules to satisfy its own thirst for power. It remains that the institutions of executive federalism could provide a region-state[58] such as Québec with a strong voice in the federation.

One of the main features of federalism is that it allows member states to maintain their own ways of life while at the same time encouraging joint activities. To borrow Samuel LaSelva's expression, federalism suggests a balance between a political desire "to live apart and to live together".[59] Another feature of federalism that we looked at earlier, namely the federal principle,[60] establishes the non-subordination of orders of government. In other words, disputes need to be settled in negotiations between equals. In a federal context, unilateralism is simply ruled out.

The non-subordination of powers among orders of government is at the heart of the vision of federalism in Québec, where there is also strong support for the principles of constitutionalism (consent, continuity, mutual recognition).[61] Respect for these principles provides assurances that changes that could directly affect Québec will not be implemented without its formal approval. As spokespersons for a national minority, Québec political leaders have always insisted on this feature of federalism since it acts as a counterweight to the will of the Canadian majority.

Elite bargaining has been repudiated over the years for excluding the people, but we may have been too swift in our condemnation.

Although we should aspire to involve the public to the greatest possible extent, it remains that political elites should not be excluded from the most sensitive negotiations on identity and citizenship since they are often the most informed.

With respect to Québec–Canada dynamics, the public debates surrounding Meech Lake and Charlottetown are taking us down a slippery slope.[62] This leads me to suggest that we not neglect negotiations that can be conducted by political elites at the level of executive federalism. Political elites and their specialized staff can serve as efficient brokers between governments and nations. In this sense, federalism is a key institution that can contribute to protecting national minorities, such as Catalonia, Scotland, Galicia and Québec, against misconceptualizations of their special needs, which are too often depicted as privileges demanded by national communities that are already spoiled rather than as legitimate claims.

Since Canada is a multinational federation, Québec's political elites seem to most stakeholders to be best positioned to speak on behalf of the Québec nation within the institutions of executive federalism. Finally, and as this book shows, every time Canada has departed from true executive federalism, it has done so at the expense of Québec interests. Common sense suggests that we reinvigorate executive federalism in Canada, for it would significantly improve democratic practices and strengthen trust in and loyalty to existing political institutions.

Executive federalism is a sign of the health of democracy in Canada. If Canadian political leaders really hope to revive Canada's shaken democratic practices, they would be well advised to place electoral reform first, offer voters an approach that is more sensitive to class differences, counter the excessive concentration of powers in the Prime Minister's Office, and find appropriate means of attenuating the inequality between different regions' influence in central institutions.

Québec's political institutions have often helped to launch major democratic reforms that have been opposed by other member states of the federation. Current debates in Québec on electoral reform, a more sensitive approach to the needs of social classes and regionalization of powers provide new avenues to explore. The Québécois are open to true executive federalism because it would allow them to discuss the pursuit of their own preferences with respect to the multination and to fortify the operation of Canada's democratic practices, which are sometimes seen as faltering. If we cannot achieve true multinational federalism, the "next best choice"[63] will be to adopt executive federalism so that Canada and Québec will be able to negotiate bilateral political solutions. In the next chapter, we will show how Canada gradually turned its back on federal practices and explain how this position has encouraged the rise of the sovereigntist movement in Québec over the last 30 years. As we will see, by seeking to portray itself as the only focus of identity, Canada has alienated the Québécois, who have in turn been concerned by the rise of majority nationalism in Canada and taken refuge in Québécois liberal nationalism.

5 The effects of majority nationalism in Canada[1]

.

> How should we view a political community that would banish one of the cultural sources that sustain it? The present awakening of nationalities is sufficient warning of the terrible conflicts unleashed in states that have scorned nations and tried to replace them, even by arbitrarily claiming nationhood themselves.[2]

There is a widespread notion, which is maintained by some intellectuals and spokespersons of the dominant political groups in Canada, according to which minority nationalism is a threat to political stability and endangers democratic practices. Eric Hobsbawm and Canadian political scientist and former federal minister Stéphane Dion are among those clearly associated with this line of thought. As a counterbalance, writers such as Michael Keating, Rainer Bauböck and James Tully, as well as former advisor to the Parti Québécois, Jean-François Lisée, have demonstrated that minority nationalism can be both socially and politically legitimate and representative. In this chapter, I will examine how majority nationalism creates obstacles to political change in Canada and encourages minority nationalism, which reacts to the ebb and flow of the dominant political order.

So far, writing on nationalism has had a tendency to focus on national minorities' quests for political independence and to neglect the nation-building activities of national majorities. In the evocative words of Rogers Brubaker, a distinction is made between "state-seeking nationalisms" and "nationalizing practices".[3] In Canada, majority nationalism is driven by all of the federal government's measures, from the Canadian Charter of Rights and Freedoms to pension benefits, the Canadian Foundatin for Innovation, the distribution of flags and the award of Millennium Chairs in education. The purpose is to promote a pan-Canadian national identity and reduce minority national feelings to expressions of folklore, when they are not seen simply as subversive elements.

The hypothesis that I would like to explore is that, given the patriation of the Constitution of Canada in 1982, the proposed Charlottetown Accord in 1992 and the Calgary Declaration in 1997, which was followed three years later by the Clarity Act, Québec has come to consider that its range of options is circumscribed, and even most often dictated, by the political power of majority nationalism. As a member-state of the federation, Québec has thus become a discontented partner in a political system that is less and less federal. Consequently, I am arguing that the Canadian federal system is knowingly and strategically discarding some of its founding features through the rejection of federal practices in many areas of politics.

In this chapter, I analyse three of these areas of politics. First, I look at Canada's Social Union Framework Agreement (SUFA, 1999–2002) with respect to how it affects the dynamics of intergovernmental relations concerning social policy. Next, I study the effects of a pan-Canadian charter of rights and freedoms that, implemented by the judicial institutions of the central power, frustrates the representativeness of Québec's National Assembly and profoundly changes the relationships between citizens and governments across Canada. Finally, I examine the growing constraints on Québec with respect to international relations.

Theoretical considerations

Based on some of my past work on the influence of political ideas, I will analyse minority–majority nationalism as an independent variable and key factor affecting politics. "Nationalism" has many meanings and can be interpreted in many ways. It is related to what Michel Foucault called a "discursive formation", or, as Craig Calhoun puts it, "a way of speaking that shapes our consciousness, but also is problematic enough that it keeps generating more issues and questions, keeps propelling us into further talk, keeps producing debates over how to think about it".[4] The term "hegemony" resonates here.

In her edifying work, *Nationalism: Five Roads to Modernity*, Liah Greenfeld analyses English, French, German, Russian and American nationalisms, and concludes that:

> The role of vanity – or desire for status – in social transformation has been largely underestimated, and greed or will to power are commonly regarded as its mainsprings. In all the five cases

> [...] the emergence of nationalism was related to preoccupation with status. The English aristocracy sought to justify it; the French and Russian nobility – to protect it; the German intellectuals – to achieve it. Even for the materialistic Americans, taxation without representation was an insult to their pride more than an injury to their economic interests. They fought – and became a nation – over respect due to them, rather than anything else.[5]

As the present chapter will illustrate, both aspiration to honour and thirst for power have also been the rule in Canada.

With respect to Canada, Jane Jenson and Sylvia Bashevkin,[6] among others, have highlighted the "world of political discourse" by asserting that focusing essentially on relations between the government and society can cause one to lose sight of the whole picture. While it might be relevant, a longitudinal study of political phenomena centring exclusively on government or society is in itself insufficient if it is not accompanied by an analysis of ideas. Political legacies are important, particularly in a federal state such as Canada, where political discourses generated by majority and minority nationalisms clash.[7]

Bashevkin considers that pan-Canadianism (which I view as a specific discourse of majority nationalism) entails a centre–left conception of the world focusing on the predominant role of the federal government. She describes this world view as the "pursuit of a more independent and distinctive Canadian in-group on the North American continent, primarily through the introduction by the federal government of specific cultural, trade and investment policies that are designed to limit US out-group influences."[8] Despite the fact that the federal government has gradually abandoned its centre–left goals and instead reduced the public sector and opened to international trade, the observation holds. Daily displays of majority nationalism in Canada can be seen in the dominant political discourse that, in the international arena, projects the image of an undifferentiated territory, proposes "national standards" in domestic policy and implies little involvement of citizens and the private sector in public affairs. This weakens Québec's ability to implement its own policies on its own territory.

As Bashevkin sees it, pan-Canadianism is based on preconceived political ideas. However, the strength of majority nationalism can also be assessed by analysing spending power and taxation, and the degree to which the contractual arrangements that establish the division of powers in a federal regime are respected.[9] This is all the more important since discussions concerning the division of powers involve intergovernmental negotiations, which leaves little room for Québec to manoeuvre. It should be noted that following the defeat of the Conservatives at the hands of Jean Chrétien's Liberals in 1993, intergovernmental negotiations became largely obsolete and were not seen as useful during the long Liberal reign from 1993 to 2006 since that government party preferred to impose its views away from the public eye, rather than legitimize them through a recognized framework for discussion.

The Canadian Charter of Rights and Freedoms only exacerbated the situation. The objective of achieving equal treatment for all citizens everywhere in Canada on the basis of universal principles has resulted, on the one hand, in an inevitable homogenization of policies across the country and, on the other hand, in a shift in the forum of political debates out of the hands of federal and provincial elected representatives and into those of judges appointed by the central government. Consequently, First Ministers' Conferences have become more or less pointless events.[10]

Moreover, it is often asserted that the repercussions of international trade limit the government's freedom of action and, therefore, its sovereignty. This has led the federal government to relieve the provinces of their jurisdiction over domestic policy. Many of the weaker provinces do not have the leverage to oppose this new trend, though stronger provinces, such as Alberta, Ontario and Québec, have regularly expressed their concerns and dissatisfaction over the years. On the one hand, the provinces are told that they will have a greater consultative role to play and broader administrative powers, but on the other hand, since they have been relieved of their jurisdiction, their so-called power is empty. In this way, member states of the Canadian federation, including Québec, are viewed as the equals of other consultative groups working in various political domains and no consideration is given to the division of powers. In such conditions, after economic globalization, what remains of sovereignty belongs to the central government. This discourse is based on a vague conception of the provinces' participation in the political process and, consequently, terms such as "collaboration", "partnership"[11] and "unity" are denuded of meaning and only strengthen the central power. Wishful thinking concerning collaboration among partisans of majority nationalism in Canada targets only the construction of a homogenous, difference-blind, national identity.

According to Rogers Brubaker, a "nationalizing state" is one that acts in the interest of and for a

> "core nation" whose language, culture, demographic position, economic welfare and political hegemony must be promoted and protected by the state. The key elements here are (1) the sense of "ownership" of the state by a particular ethnocultural nation that is conceived as distinct from the citizen or permanent resident population as a whole, and (2) the "remedial" or compensatory project of using state power to promote the core nation's specific (and heretofore inadequately served) interests.[12]

In contrast, Québécois minority nationalism, which is represented by all of the political parties sitting in the Québec National Assembly and speaks with a single voice in Ottawa through the Bloc Québécois, has little power in its attempts to make Québec's political aspirations concrete in the form of public policies and to gain recognition for the distinct nature of Québec society. Faced with a central state employing nationalistic practices, these political parties are reduced to acting defensively, while partisans of majority nationalism undermine liberalism and express their vision in terms of national unity.

After this theoretical interlude, we will now take a brief look at three areas of politics that generate major tensions between Québec and the central government. Conflict deepened with the return of the Liberals in 1993 after ten years in opposition, but since Stephen Harper's Conservatives came to power in Ottawa in January 2006, greater openness to Québec's claims has been expressed.

Three government initiatives

The following inquiry concerns federal government policies in fields as diverse as social policy, the constitutional entrenchment of the Charter of Rights and Freedoms, and international relations since the early 1980s. Its purpose is to show how Brubaker's description of the nationalism practices of Central and Eastern European countries can also be applied to Canada.[13]

The Canadian Social Union

The Social Union is a prime example of a concerted effort to transform areas of political competency from the top down with no respect for the division of powers. In other words, the federal government considers the Canadian Social Union a "tool of statecraft".[14]

The idea of a social union in Canada appeared publicly in the wake of the failure of the Meech Lake Accord (1987–1990), during the time that constitutional discussions were taking place concerning the federal proposals of September 1991.[15] Initially, Ottawa saw the idea as an instrument necessary for nation building. Later, it was seen as a means for the member states of the federation to fully shoulder their responsibilities with respect to social policy and to put joint claims to the central government through intergovernmental negotiations. After gains and losses in federal–provincial relations, the social union idea was finally merged with the plan for majority nationalism blind to the distinctions of existing jurisdictions. The fact that "money talks" cast a shadow on earlier constitutional agreements, thus favouring the deep pockets of the central government.

Everything flows from recognition of the federal spending power because only member states who acknowledge it have access to federal generosity. The right to opt out with full financial compensation now no longer exists for the provinces unless they meet strict conditions set by Ottawa. The central government, which reserves the right to contribute to provincial budgets, provides compensation on two conditions: first, that the provinces do everything in their power to achieve pan-Canadian healthcare, post-secondary education, social assistance and social services objectives, all of which are under exclusive provincial jurisdiction; and, second, that they agree in good faith to respect the division of responsibilities approved by Ottawa and the provinces, except for Québec.[16] As Will Kymlicka explains:

> If language rights and social entitlements should be nation-wide in scope, then decisions about them must be made at the federal rather than provincial level – i.e., in a forum where English-speaking Canadians form an overwhelming majority. [...]
>
> So, the idea that Canadians form a single nation from sea to sea, and that the federal government should promote this common nationhood, has increased the mobility and political power of English-speaking Canadians. It is not surprising that English-speaking Canadians have so strongly adopted this pan-Canadian nationalism.[17]

Continuing in this vein, Alain Noël says that Québec's only means of expressing disagreement is to add a footnote to compulsory federal programmes.[18] This is the end of a federalism that was based on real collaboration among member states and, more significantly, between member states and the federal government.[19]

Moreover, the central government has decreed that it can now take new initiatives through the Social Union Framework Agreement on the condition that it gives provincial and territorial governments three months' notice. Its means consist of direct transfers to individuals and organizations involved in healthcare, post-secondary education, social assistance and social services. In this case, what is in question is not only one of the most controversial changes to the division of powers in Canada, but a transformation that contradicts the country's multinational composition and replaces it with mononational federalism in accordance with the central government's intentions. As we saw in Chapter 2, the central government continues to undermine the normative considerations at the heart of federalism and to impose its domineering views with little concern for the national communities in question.

"Change by non-constitutional means" has become the phrase of the day in Ottawa where central government initiatives have resulted in nothing less than significant constitutional modifications.[20] The changes are global and structural, and also set precedents that will have to be taken into account in federal–provincial affairs. However, Québec still bears the burden of proving to its partners in the federation that a mockery has once again been made of the federal principle. Indeed, this might someday backfire on Ottawa, as Jennifer Smith explains:

> [T]he tradition and the [federal] principle remain benchmarks by which to evaluate the state of federalism in the country. These benchmarks can serve to delegitimize non-constitutional, anti-federal change.
> [...] The federal principle is a critical component of democracy in large states. This is why it ought not to be jettisoned in series of developments that mount up to informal constitutional change. The more important the principle, the greater the need for formal process of change.[21]

Study of social policy confirms the thesis that the central government wishes to impose its centralizing views notwithstanding the Canadian constitution. This is done under the cover of "cooperative federalism", a euphemism invented in the 1960s to soften the appearance of domineering federalism.

The entrenchment of the Canadian Charter of Rights and Freedoms

The central government's most overt action in the direction of pan-Canadian nationalism was probably the constitutional entrenchment of the Charter of Rights and Freedoms, considered the key component of the 1982 patriation. Entrenching rights broke with the Canadian legal and constitutional order,[22] and imposing the Charter interfered with the supremacy of the provincial and federal legislatures. In effect, the Charter's insertion into the Constitution, to which Québec has still not consented, was not only a change in the division of powers in Canada, but, even more importantly, a reworking of federal practices. So far, this is the central government's least disguised nationalist initiative.

Combined with official multiculturalism and bilingualism, the Charter of Rights and Freedoms, which was the personal work of Pierre Elliott Trudeau, was the keystone for a universal basis for a pan-Canadian identity. For Trudeau,[23] a legal nation, in which every citizen has a set of individual rights, is the institutional expression of a "just society", for it is based on reason instead of the "parochial" and "emotional" ties of the regional entities on which Canada was built.[24] The individual rights regime established by the Charter can be considered one of the most virulent attacks on Québec's legislative power because it scorns Québec's interpretations of federalism. James Tully accurately describes the nationalist implication of the Charter in these words:

> When the Quebec Assembly seek to preserve and enhance Quebec's character as a modern, predominantly French-speaking society, it finds that its traditional sovereignty in this area is capped by a Charter in terms of which all its legislation must be phrased and justified, but from which any recognition of Quebec's distinct character has been completely excluded. The effect of the Charter is thus to assimilate Quebec to a pan-Canadian national culture, exactly what the 1867 constitution, according to Lord Watson, was established to prevent. Hence, from this perspective, the Charter is "imperial" in the precise sense of the term that has always been used to justify independence.[25]

Rights are pre-political goods, and consequently the government responsible for defining them comes out the winner in political conflicts in a federal system. According to Guy Laforest, federalists' failure to found the nation on a charter of rights is partly a result of the fact that, unlike the Québec nation, the expression of which was maintained and largely modernized during the Quiet Revolution, the English-Canadian nation has been essentially a creation of the central government ever since Confederation.[26] Thus, the central government has always represented the Canadian nation; Canadian identity, in other words, the nationalist expression of the majority, permeates the spirit of the central government.[27] The Charter can therefore be interpreted as a direct response to the growing influence of the Québec government in defining and developing the Québec nation. Through a rights regime, the central government determines which ties of allegiance should be acknowledged by the citizens of Canada.

According to Peter Russell, the Charter has three unifying, nationalist components.[28] First, it is a unifying symbol because its audience, attentive to discourse on rights and shared values, is composed of all Canadians, from coast to coast. This symbolic function is essential to the definition of Canadian citizenship and identity. Second, the Charter promotes national criteria and thus standardizes policies so that they comply with these criteria. The language policies are a clear example of this. Finally, a consequence of the judicialization of the Canadian political system is that political issues are no longer defined regionally or deliberated in provincial legislatures because they become "national" and non-territorial. This is strengthened by the fact that the Canadian judicial system is hierarchical and the Supreme Court's case law is enforceable with respect to all other courts. Guy Laforest takes this argument even further when he notes that

> the 1982 Charter deterritorializes conflicts; it takes them out of provincial boundaries and places them in a pan-Canadian juridico-political arena where they will be judged in the court of last appeal by a Supreme Court that belongs to the central government.[29]

Furthermore, Laforest claims that the Charter, in addition to standardizing some social practices, encourages the convergence of the Civil Code of Québec – a key component of Québec's different status in Canada – and common law, thereby reducing one of the features that makes Québec a distinct society in the Canadian whole.

A corollary of the nationalist functions of the Charter is an undermining of the federal origins of the country. While the foundations of the federal system are intrinsically based on regional and territorial boundaries, the Charter changes the rules of the political game by obscuring territorial specificity, which then becomes insignificant, and substituting a framework in which all identities, minorities or not, territorial or not, are equivalent. The entrance of non-territorial groups and individuals active in the Canadian national community into the political arena has diluted the principle of "two majorities" defended by most political and social players in Québec. In other words, the dominant nationalism expressed by the Charter views other identities as de facto minorities. Québec, now a province among the others according to the new rules, is limited in its ability to promote a set of values and shared priorities that are different from those of the other provinces.

Janet Hiebert has done an empirical study of interpretations and applications of the Charter in order to see whether it weakens the territorial pluralism of Canadian federalism or permits provincial diversity in political deliberations.[30] Without describing in detail the various legal issues on which her study sheds light, let us note that among her conclusions is the observation that most of the Supreme Court's decisions have interpreted the Charter in a manner consistent with federal diversity. From this she concludes that the Court's reasons in defence of the provinces' interests attenuate the Charter's centralizing tendencies. While she does not go so far as to say that the Charter has no effect on provincial diversity in the political process, Hiebert claims that there is no empirical evidence for the thesis that Charter case law has produced a standardized interpretation of rights with no regard for regional differences. Nonetheless, Hiebert adds a major and revealing proviso:

> The Charter poses the greatest constraint on provincial autonomy when legislation is in direct conflict with a protected right that is specific in its definition. [...] However, the majority of protected rights are stated in vague and abstract terms. Therefore the constraint on Quebec's capacity to determine school language instruction policy should not serve as the basis for a general proposition that the pursuit of cultural objectives or community values by provinces will inevitably be vetoed by the Charter.[31]

According to Hiebert, the basis for the Court's decisions is the fact that the "reasonable limits" clause in section 1 of the Charter is explicitly interpreted in a federal manner. In other words, the limits placed on the rights regime are precisely those that make the Charter compatible with federalism. From this point of view, the provinces can use political initiatives as major instruments for countering the

Charter's individualistic effects on the condition that the values they embody are consistent with a free and democratic society. The fact that governments have to shoulder the burden of proving the fairness of their objectives is considered perfectly in accordance with the principle of provincial diversity, while the notwithstanding clause (section 33 of the Charter), the spirit of which should express provincial diversity even better, is stained with illegitimacy to the point of restricting its use by provincial governments in a political culture that is increasingly legalistic.

While Hiebert's study makes a major empirical contribution to the debate over the Charter's compatibility with federalism, it does not affect the assertion that the Charter is contrary to the spirit of federalism and inconsistent with Canadian constitutional practices. First, as Hiebert admits, the case law on provincial diversity is rather limited, and this is not a simple question of statistics. It is quite possible that the effects of the Charter are felt long before any cases come to court; for example, when governments draft policies in such a way that they will comply with the Charter a priori. The Charter's standardizing tendency therefore cannot be shown by analysing case law alone. In other words, if standardization can take place prior to court cases, then a more accurate examination of the effects of the Charter must begin with an analysis of the political process. By looking only downstream and at a relatively small body of case law, Hiebert can claim that the Charter does not excessively favour the central government, but by doing so she overlooks the standardizing and centralizing effects of the Charter, which weigh heavily upstream, where legislators try to avoid conflicts. Instead of clarifying the Charter's repercussions, therefore, Hiebert's methodological choice obscures them.

Second, even if we admit that section 1 of the Charter is an asset to the provinces, the latter are nonetheless responsible for stating their intentions and justifying their actions before a central institution. Majority nationalism may be operating through insinuation, but it is nonetheless a fact that a central institution has the final word in areas under exclusive provincial jurisdiction.[32]

Third, as Rainer Knopff and Fred Morton point out, the central government is in a win–win situation. On one hand, if the provinces lose before the Court, there is reduction in provincial diversity and the establishment of a standardized framework for provincial policy initiatives. On the other hand, if the central government loses, a central institution, namely the federal judicial apparatus that interprets the federal Charter of Rights and has deliberative authority across the whole country, will still emerge as the winner. For the central government, a lost case is a lost case, nothing more, while for the provinces a lost case severely limits their ability to experiment with policies in their jurisdictions and to adapt them to the specific needs of their people. The feeling that Canadians have non-territorial rights is strengthened every time the Court is asked to rule on a Charter issue, which provides the central government with a legal arsenal for use in future conflicts with the provinces.[33] What will happen to regional diversity and experimentation, the bedrock of federalism? Once again, the Charter looks like a non-federal document with consequences that are considerably more negative for the provinces when they lose cases than for the central government when the provinces win.

Finally, the Charter is redundant if the purpose is to affirm that section 1 promotes federal diversity. As Knopff and Morton argue, if diversity alone sufficed as the criterion of reasonableness, then the Charter really would be null. The problem can be summarized as follows: if the meaning of rights is vague and open to the different interpretations of member states of the federation, then why not give the provinces the right to differ in their interpretations of basic rights? Indeed, Québec promulgated its own Charter of Human Rights and Freedoms[34] before the Canadian Charter was entrenched. It thus showed that, like most western countries, it could require itself to respect basic human rights. Why should its legislature not be responsible for enforcing respect for the rights of its citizens in its areas of jurisdiction? The answer can be found precisely in the nation-building endeavour of the central government, which acts as the sole guardian of citizens' rights across the country, thus protecting individuals from the "connotations of the capriciousness" of provincial governments, particularly that of Québec, which aspires to play a major role in the area.

International relations

What is at stake in international relations is not the positioning of the Québec state in external affairs since Québec's positions on refugees, peace missions, NORAD, NATO, the war on terror and other areas that are clearly under federal jurisdiction are generally in agreement with those of Canada. What is in question is the possibility for Québec to expand its responsibilities in its own areas of jurisdiction to the international level. As Panayotis Soldatos and Daniel Latouche[35] have noted, Québec's presence in international relations takes the form of parallel diplomacy of sub-state stakeholders, and less frequently takes the traditional avenues of state players.[36]

Québec abides by the Gérin–Lajoie doctrine, which has the advantage of being simple, that was adopted by the Walloon and Flemish governments at the time of the major institutional reforms that transformed Belgium from a unitary state into a federal state. Concretely, it involves gaining endorsement for the extension of a federated state's domestic jurisdiction into the international arena. This means that a member-state of a federation would be able to expand its responsibilities (e.g. concerning culture, education, language and healthcare) to the international scene.[37] Consensus on this proposal was reached quickly in Québec, and is still a guiding theme and even a pillar of the Québec autonomy movement.[38]

The politicians and "mandarins" of the Canadian government have seen this as a desire to cast a shadow on Canada abroad, which has led to clashes with the central government, particularly with respect to the Francophonie and especially under the governments of prime ministers Trudeau and Chrétien, for whom Canada's foreign policy could not be shared with any of the member states of the Canadian federation. The federal attitude changed slightly under Brian Mulroney's government, from 1984 to 1993, and since January 2006 under Stephen Harper's minority government. While the Conservatives and Liberals agree on the broad directions to follow in international relations, the role that Québec hopes to play in the Francophonie and in international organizations poses a problem. For example, when Laurent Fabius visited Canada in November 1984, two months after the Progressive-Conservative Party had defeated the Liberal Party, Brian Mulroney noted:

> The Government of Canada intends to fully exercise its constitutional responsibilities with regards to international relations. However, we consider it normal and desirable that the Government of Quebec maintains relations with France, justified by Quebec's cultural identity. We recognize the legitimacy of direct and privileged relations between Paris and Quebec, as long as they respect and deal with areas that do not clash with federal jurisdictions.[39]

However, with respect to relations with the United States, the central government, even under the Conservatives in 1984–1993, has tended to keep the Québec government as distant as possible, and has intervened in this sense.[40] As soon as the Conservatives were defeated in

Ottawa in 1993, the Liberal government quickly returned to its line of pursuing a single and unique foreign policy, denying the provinces any role in international relations, even in cases where culture, education and social issues were at stake. Québec has been more disadvantaged than the other member states of the federation by this return to the central government's traditional Liberal line because it is the province that has tried hardest to exercise its international powers in these areas over the years.[41]

After Québec's 1995 referendum, Ottawa launched a series of initiatives designed to place greater limitations on Québec's presence in international fora. Influenced by what has been described as "Plan B", the central government developed a *containment policy* with the firm intention of removing Québec leaders from the international scene. A number of examples can be given, such as the invitation extended in 1998 to Louise Beaudoin, Québec Minister of Culture and Communication, by Sheila Copps, federal Minister of Canadian Heritage, to participate in an international conference on culture but without the right to intervene.[42]

The containment policy was also vigorously pursued at the Summit of the Americas in April 2001, when neither the Premier of Québec nor any minister of the Québec government was permitted to make a speech or public presentation of any sort before the 34 heads of state meeting in the capital city of Québec.[43] The federal position has relaxed slightly since Stephen Harper's Conservatives arrived in January 2006, in that Québec has been given a spot in the Canadian delegation to UNESCO, but this is still far from the Gérin–Lajoie doctrine or the roles accorded to regions such as Flanders and Wallonia[44] in international relations.

A case for a multidimensional approach

At the international conference that led to publication of *Multinational Democracies*,[45] a number of authors, including Guy Laforest, David Miller and James Tully, opened the way to an avant-garde, multidimensional analysis of democratic multinational societies. Comparative political science and political philosophy were combined to shed new light on power relations and the stakes related to governance. I believe this is a significant advance towards understanding contemporary political phenomena and that it should be pursued. On the basis of recent research, I also believe that another area needs to be taken into consideration: government policy.

The centralizing and non-constitutional directions of political decisions made by the Government of Canada can be seen more clearly through an approach that integrates research on international relations with traditional models of comparative politics. Robert Keohane's[46] discussion of hegemonic stability in political contexts where constitutional guarantees are not clearly delimited is another step towards understanding the motivations and incentives for cooperation and collaboration in a federal system increasingly defined by the decrees of a central hegemony.

In other words, Canadian federalism can be compared to a system of each for their own: if they do not want to participate in a specific pan-Canadian policy, member states have no choice other than to purely and simply declare sovereignty. If cooperation involves non-compliance with constitutional mechanisms in intergovernmental relations, as is suggested by the above statement, then the principle of "alignment of interests", which was initially supposed to support the desire to cooperate, is maintained by a domineering player that defines interests, imposes them on weaker partners and does not care whether there is mutual agreement or the consent of all stakeholders. In a context of true collaboration, member states can opt out if they have no interest in cooperation. However, in the present federal system, constitutional obstacles exclude this option. The federal system is increasingly restrictive.

The state of collaboration in Canada corresponds to the theory of hegemonic stability in that the central government establishes the parameters for cooperation using incentives and sanctions. Collaboration in such a federation is comparable to cooperation dictated by hegemonic stability in international relations that, according to Robert Keohane, "relies on a dominant power making rules and providing incentives for others to conform with those rules".[47] Consequently, collaboration and compromise imply a system of negotiation in which the parties are authorized to collaborate and to make compromises. However, as Alain Noël explains, "[w]hen the promotion of a common interest is automatically obtained and does not demand mutual adjustments, coordination or negotiations, there is no need to collaborate".[48] Thus, the decrees of majority nationalism, not the members who participate in negotiations, define what is in the public interest in Canada. If cooperation is a political game, this is not true of a preconceived, unassailable thesis that central power ensures harmony. When cooperation emerges from intergovernmental negotiations, it is often because little regard is paid to Québec's consent, which is considered unnecessary. This is what happened with the Social Union Framework Agreement: essentially, the final text retained only the line of thought of federal public servants.

In the present situation, one of the ways that majority nationalism is expressed is in the fact that a number of provinces have less desire to develop their own provincial policies than to get themselves heard in the planning of pan-Canadian policies, and they do not challenge the pan-Canadian nature of those policies. Provincial governments share the opinion that citizens trust Ottawa on these issues. We are now seeing rivalry between provincial governments to gain the highest "visibility" in their citizens' eyes through cooperation in their areas of jurisdiction. However, it should be noted that, from one area of cooperation to the next, the provincial electorates form a whole: the provinces, unlike sovereign states, thus have no worries about the effects of cooperation on various electorates that are formally divided. This point is important because, on the one hand, it increases the central government's motivation to act like a hegemon and, on the other hand, it provides that same government with the legitimacy to act in this way in the eyes of the majority of Canadians. Consequently, the theory of hegemonic leadership is not based on power alone, as it is in international relations, but can also be carried in majority domination, which is more difficult to challenge because the "opt-out" option is not as available as it is in the complex assembly of interstate relations. This reasoning is instructive in that it concerns the future of federal practices in Canada, for how can a member state challenge a hegemon if the majority of the country and nine provinces out of ten perceive it as making a legitimate proposal? Is cooperation (or "collaboration") possible if it is not based from the beginning on an overlap of interests, as is presupposed in theories of international cooperation?

The three cases studied in this chapter show that Québec's ability to set its own international policy, like its domestic policy, is increasingly hindered and even reduced in the name of Canada's "national interest". Ottawa is behaving as if it alone personifies Canadian identity,[49] and affirms that it is the only entity mandated to act in that way. In short, this is the ultimate expression of the majority nationalism that federal politicians are trying to impose on all.

Ottawa's attempts to avoid taking the provinces into account have included deciding upon new reforms through direct consultation with individuals and concerned groups. On the basis of this model, the central government holds that it is the only government able to express the interests of all Canadians, no matter what the political issue and, by extension, no matter what the jurisdiction. Consequently, "collaboration" and "partnership" are terms used only to mask a situation in which the provinces, in particular Québec, cannot expect any constitutional discussion because that would imply confrontation and rivalry, and that is not, according to federal politicians, "what Canadians want". End of discussion. As we have seen in Chapter 4, this is how executive federalism is challenged by the central government, which hopes not to have to face the provinces and debate the legitimacy of players and political actions.

In the course of his reflections on the federal government's role with respect to new reproductive technologies (NRT), this type of attitude has led Will Kymlicka to point out a major failure:

> The problem, of course, is that (true) federalism puts serious limits on the extent to which English Canadians can act on this national identity. The only way for English Canadians to act collectively in an area like NTRs is to undermine the federal principles which have made it possible for Quebeckers to act collectively. In other words, the impasse in Quebec–Canada relationships is not simply that Quebeckers have developed a strong sense of political identity which is straining the bonds of federalism. The problem is also that Canadians outside Quebec have developed a strong sense of pan-Canadian political identity that strains the boundaries of federalism. [...] This suggests that if we want to unravel the paradoxes of Quebec's national identity, we need to look more honestly at the development of English Canada's political identity.[50]

It seems more than appropriate to note here an essential point in the Supreme Court of Canada's Reference Re. the Secession of Québec. In paragraph 66, the Court ruled that:

> The relationship between democracy and federalism means, for example, that in Canada there may be different and equally legitimate majorities in different provinces and territories and at the federal level. No one majority is more or less "legitimate" than the others as an expression of democratic opinion. [...] A federal system of government enables different provinces to pursue policies responsive to the particular concerns and interests of people in that province...

What are we to conclude from this? Only that Canada strongly imposes majority nationalism by, on the one hand, rejecting federal practices and, on the other hand, accusing Québec's statespersons of destabilizing the country, all without showing any signs of remorse. Let us go back to Brubaker: the dominant group's nationalistic practices have never been so strong in Canada, and this decreases Québec's trust in institutions that are less and less easy to call "federal". In *Reimagining Canada*, Jeremy Webber remarks to his great dismay following the failure of the Charlottetown Accord (1992) that, after all the negotiations in Canada to respond to Québec's claims, "not one [constitutional] amendment had addressed the traditional concerns of Quebec with the spending power, the division of powers, disallowance, or the recognition of Quebec's distinctiveness".[51]

In sum, the impoverishment of federalism in Canada has strengthened minority nationalisms. The lack of openness to the Québécois and First Nations is causing national communities to gradually turn their backs on the Canadian government and begin developing political and social plans that are more in tune with their demands. This makes it urgent to think differently about power relations and especially to think about Canadian federalism in multinational terms so as not to betray the way that national communities see themselves and thereby risk further wearing away the cement binding the Canadian whole. That would compromise Canada's future. In the last chapter, we will concentrate on thinking about a multinational Canada with a view to strengthening democratic practices through full and complete recognition of the nations that live there.

6 Resistance and potential

The duty to consider the multination[1]

A decent society is one whose institutions do not humiliate people.[2]

The concepts of "multination", "multinational democracy" and "multinational federation" have gained prominence in academic circles over the last decade. Democratic multinational federations are characterized by a propensity to reflect deep diversity and maintain stability even though significant tensions may exist. Unlike non-democratic multinational federations, these are better able to pass the test of time through appropriate management of politics and freely negotiated power sharing. Most democratic multinational federations, such as Belgium, Canada and Switzerland,[3] have faced different types of challenges over the years. These three federations have proven to be relatively stable under different conditions of stress. There are also other types of democratic multinational federations. The United Kingdom and Spain, for example, offer an additional basis for comparison as "unions of states", to use Murray Forsyth's terminology.

As we have seen in this book, the Canadian experiment is possibly one of the least stable democratic multinational federations. This is due largely to a stronger identity quest on the part of the Québécois in response to inadequate representation of Québec by the central government and to the unwillingness of other member states of the Canadian federation to fully recognize Québec as a political nation.

Following the Meech Lake debacle of 1990, the discussions leading to the failed Charlottetown Accord of 1992, and the Québec referendum of 1995 and its aftermath, the concept of "multinational federation" has gained popularity. During this period of especially high tension, the notion of "multinational federation" has also been attacked many times in circles that claim to be "federalist" although they are in reality Canadian nationalist milieus of purely Jacobin inspiration.

Canadian colleagues, such as John Meisel and Jean Laponce, have been among the scholars most at ease with the concept of the multination as a means of depicting the Canadian political community and, above all, with defending it as a real option for managing diversity in Canada. This is probably due to their great familiarity with Europe, which has been the focus of their work. Other Canadian colleagues, such as Philip Resnick and Alan Cairns, have also been quite receptive to the idea but have insisted that if the concept is to be applied, it is clear that political powers gained at the level of the nation (i.e. Québec) will have to be lost at the central level (i.e. Ottawa). As we saw in Chapter 3, Canadian nationalists have considered the notion of multinational federation to be un-Canadian, divisive and detrimental to the future of the country, and have even interpreted such an approach as sowing the seeds of secession.

In English Canada and Québec, members of the Research Group on Multinational Societies have been strong proponents of multinational federalism for Canada. They point out, however, that if Québec were to secede it would face the same issue, since there are 11 Aboriginal nations on its territory.

We should examine three bodies of literature in order to better describe the challenges facing emerging multinational federations before making general proposals concerning promising avenues for research and political action. More specifically, the literature can be grouped around three frameworks of reference: John Rawls' "cooperative scheme in perpetuity", Daniel Elazar's "self rule plus shared-rules" and Ernest Renan's "daily plebiscite".

In light of the country's historical foundations and contemporary constitutional and political developments, I intend to assess the extent to which these authors provide accurate theoretical understanding relevant to management of diversity in Canada as well as useful insights for countries such as Spain and Belgium.

John Rawls' cooperative scheme in perpetuity

The first body of literature that inspires most policymakers concerned with the integrity of the Canadian state, particularly since the early 1970s, builds on the work of liberal philosopher John Rawls. Rawls presented his vision of the world as a "cooperative scheme in perpetuity". He proposed the establishment of a fair distribution of wealth and power in liberal democracies; however, in the end, his position can be seen as an abstract theory of simple distribution.

The liberal system proposed by Rawls is portrayed as protecting individual rights while at the same time giving the state the power to intervene if actions prevent other people from pursuing their own goals in life (in other words, directly threaten the principle of equal liberty) or if the allocation of resources increases the hardship suffered by those who are already less well off in society (in other words, challenges the difference principle).

It is clear from this brief sketch of Rawls' basic framework for a just liberal order that his understanding of politics applies more readily to unitary states and communities that are homogeneous, as well as to states that build on territorial federalism – the United States constituting his ideal type. Rawls does not raise the question of the contours of identity and does not examine the operation of complex states. His work is on another level, prior to any conflict between national communities. His work is ahistorical but nonetheless hugely influential in political theory.

The "cooperative scheme in perpetuity" turns a blind eye to the fact that societies are often fragmented along lines of gender, social class, regional membership, religion and language, and that it is above all necessary to find means to adjust to and reflect diversity rather than force groups to achieve unwanted unity. In his early writings, Rawls noted: "the boundaries of these schemes are given by the notion of a self-contained national community."[4]

The notion of a "cooperative scheme in perpetuity" projects an image of control and containment much more that of free deliberation and open process, which are necessary for communities in pluralist societies to be free and to choose their futures in a democratic manner. Like James Tully, and as I have shown throughout this book, I favour a vision of politics based on respect for other communities and open to negotiation.

The Canadian centralizers who are busily erecting roadblocks to the establishment of a multinational federalism that would deal with the problems inherent to Canada's federation look to Rawls' theoretical defence of fair liberal principles in the context of national homogeneity in order to legitimize their monolithic vision of the nation-state. According to their interpretation, a fair liberal state has to be neutral with respect to mediating demands made by all groups in the state, regardless of their status (i.e. social and ethnic groups are interchangeable with national minorities).

Many Canadian political scientists have drawn upon the political model put forth by Rawls and his orthodox liberal followers to reject Québec's aspirations for a different status within the federation, and have argued that to say otherwise would take us down a slippery slope to secession.[5] Jeremy Webber, a jurist by profession, has expressed his opposition to this argument, commenting that such a position makes discussion among political leaders impossible. For Webber, this type of argument is a non-starter in a democratic regime, federal or not.

> Those who resist all accommodation assume that political allegiance naturally tends to be single. They therefore refuse concessions to local allegiances and emphasise a single, central allegiance in order to maintain commitment to the whole. In doing so, however, they suggest, usually implicitly but sometimes explicitly, that minority communities have to be ready to weaken their commitment to their local communities in the interest of the whole – that Quebecers must be Canadians first, that they should choose between Quebec and Canada.[6]

Canadian nationalists have developed ingenious arguments draped in Rawlsian language about the "cooperative scheme in perpetuity", but why draw on this scheme in the first place? On what normative principles are such arguments based? What values provide the foundations for perpetual cooperation, and what interests are the proponents of this school of thought defending? These questions remain largely unanswered and need clarification.

Note that Rawls developed his theoretical framework based only on the United States, which is a prime example of territorial federalism. If Rawls' analysis is blindly transposed onto a multinational situation, his interpretation will be inappropriate and problematic because its implications could be harmful to minority national communities.[7]

From a very different perspective, one based on the principle of nationality, David Miller elaborates a typology of three forms of social division that can be identified within a political community, namely ethnic cleavages, rival nationalities and, his personal contribution, nested identities. The first type, ethnic cleavages, illustrates segmentation in a political community. In many ways, and in contrast to what Kymlicka has pointed out elsewhere, one can argue that this is a more accurate description of Switzerland than is the "multinational pattern". The second type, rival nationalities, applies to separate, inward-looking, exclusive groups. Cyprus, Israel and the former Czechoslovakia are all examples that spring to mind. The third type, nested nationalities, can be found when territorially based political communities are encompassed within a single "nation", understood here as a "nation-state". According to Miller, cases in point include the Basque country, Catalonia, Galicia, Scotland, Wales, Flanders, Wallonia, Québec and many other small nations that often have dual identities.

Miller's typology is not naive. It is motivated by a desire to abandon the use of the term "nation" to describe nations without formal statehood. By his own admission,

> the label matters because of the power of the idea of national self-determination. Once it is conceded that a territorial community genuinely constitutes a nation, we seem already to have shown that there is good reason for the community in question to be granted political autonomy.[8]

In reaction to this type of argument, I would stress that the right to name oneself is an act of empowerment and an expression of political freedom to which constitutive nations of multinational democratic federations have a right. This right was exercised in the June 2006 referendum in Catalonia.

For authors such as Miller, democratic multinational federations are antinomic and fall into his second category, namely that of rival nationalities. Although Miller is sensitive to the presence of diverse ethno-cultural groups in a territory and "nested identities", he simply pursues the "cooperative scheme in perpetuity". Miller goes on to argue that Belgian, Canadian, Spanish and Swiss nationalities are singular because each is based on a long-established cultural and political association. Owing to their co-existence with an encompassing nation it would be inconceivable, according to Miller, for the members of such an association to see themselves as constituting something other than a sub-set of an established polity. He gives three reasons for this: "cultural overlap", "mutual economic advantage" and an "interwoven history".[9] In his view, no one can disentangle what has been interlocked over the years through exchanges of various kinds. In other words, the communities are prisoners of one another, clearly reminiscent of a cooperative scheme in perpetuity. Finally, from this angle, secession is simply a non-option for members of constitutive nations since their members are inextricably intertwined with an existing nation-state.

While Miller's contribution is based on an in-depth historical analysis, it flows mainly from a set of observations concerning British society. Moreover, there is disagreement over the implications of his analysis, which produces contradictory readings of his work. Indeed, Rawls' arguments are often more striking and difficult to rebut because they are theoretical propositions with no empirical ties. Thus, Rawls' conclusions are difficult to falsify and are most often used by political players for ideological purposes in order to keep regimes in place without worrying very much about issues of democracy or the misrepresentation of national communities. Yet it is important today, perhaps more than at any other time in modern history, to propose political models capable of both recognition and openness. Daniel Elazar's work on uses of federalism and Renan's legacy encouraging routine deliberation are promising possibilities for strengthening democracy in complex societies. We will turn to these now.

Daniel Elazar's self-rule and shared rule

The second body of literature that I want to focus on is composed of contributions surrounding the influential work of Daniel Elazar, and more pointedly his depiction of "self-rule plus shared rule"[10] as a way towards solutions to conflicts that undermine community relations in multinational federations. Essentially, Elazar is speaking of the combined need for autonomy and the quest for solidarity as a way to properly manage diversity. With respect to potential conflict management in multinational federations, it is clear that the balance between self-rule and shared rule is central and requires our attention.

Elazar portrays the federal principle as a founding pillar of modern democratic states and as an insurance policy that allows communities to further develop their democratic practices. In *Exploring Federalism*, Elazar argues that the federal goal is not centralization but rather non-centralization. In that book, Elazar provides logical reasons for the need to distribute powers among several centres so that no centre can dominate the agenda and permanently impose its views on the others.[11] For Elazar, this condition is contractual and guarantees respect for all members in a federal compact.

Note that Elazar has had a major influence on members of the Comparative Federalism and Federation Research Committee of the International Political Science Association. Robert Agranoff, Michael Burgess, John Kincaid, Ronald Watts and many others have benefited from his writings and have further elaborated on his work.

I have defined federalism as a political device for establishing viable institutions and flexible relationships capable of facilitating interstate relations, intrastate linkages and intercommunity relations.[12] Inspired by Elazar, I have also warned in this book against the dangers of "nationalizing" central governments since doing so weakens federal practices. What is at stake concerns power relationships and the extent to which the central government is sufficiently democratic so as not to act as a hegemon, even in cases where it has the capacity to flex its muscles and display its political strength.

The central government's desire for additional powers in multinational federal settings has often led to a growing inclination on the part of member states to opt out of the federation, especially when ethnic fragmentation matches state boundaries. This is the situation in which Québec finds itself.

What this suggests is that, at the very least, central governments in democratic multinational federations must exert a high level of restraint. Echoing Elazar, Robert Agranoff has very aptly described this phenomenon:

> The federal idea is not a centralizing principle, but a non-centralizing one. While it may require a whole body of one people or the importance of the federation as a general commitment, an all-powerful centre is not the core idea.[13]

The desire on the part of majority nations in multinational federations to centralize has rarely led to the implementation of policies favouring diversity and has frequently been accompanied by political tensions. Opposition by member states is easy to understand considering that such initiatives are meant to homogenize economic, political and social practices and undermine the roles of member states in the federal pact. Historical legacy becomes a non-issue since what matters is the *hic et nunc* and, for central public officials, it is simply unfortunate if the member states of a given multinational federation see the original compact eroded on a day-to-day basis. As long as the centre holds and can impose its will, everything will be fine. *But for how long?* one may ask.

This leads me to the following question: can the centre hold for the long term under conditions that are strained due to inadequate recognition of the nations making up the federation? Charles Taylor argues that if

> a uniform model of citizenship fits better the American image of the liberal state, it is also true that this is a straitjacket for many political societies. The world needs other models to be legiti-

mized, in order to allow for more humane and less constraining modes of political cohabitation.[14]

Taylor's contribution, which was described in Chapter 3, is central to any attempt to take national diversity into account and constitutes a major theoretical advance for those fighting injustice and unfairness.

Other political philosophers have continued in Taylor's direction. Will Kymlicka, for one, has opened up a major field of research by distinguishing special representation rights from political rights, to be granted respectively to polyethnic communities and to national groups within existing countries, multinational or not. This has contributed to the notion that there are new ways in which political communities can continue to reside in multinational federations.

Kymlicka argues that polyethnic rights are

> intended to help ethnic groups and religious minorities express their cultural particularity and pride without it hampering their success in the economic and political institutions of the dominant society. [...] Unlike self-government rights, polyethnic rights are usually intended to promote integration into the larger society, not self-government.[15]

He goes on to establish, and this is highly relevant to our discussion, that

> Multination federalism divides people into separate "peoples," each with its own historic rights, territories, and powers of self-government; and each, therefore with its own political community. They may view their own political community as primary, and the value and authority of the larger federation as derivative.[16]

Since they are characterized by societal diversity, federal societies constitute a propitious setting for multinationalism. To quote Kymlicka, "federalism can provide meaningful self-government for a national minority, guaranteeing its ability to make decisions in certain areas without being outvoted by the larger society".[17] However, it should be mentioned that in the Canadian case, Québec's capacity for self-government has been seriously eroded, especially during the last decade (see Chapters 4 and 5). Indeed, the central government has taken many actions to diminish or at least constrain the power that national minorities can exercise, with a view to rallying individuals' allegiance towards the centre.

In the Canadian context, this can be illustrated by the proliferation of federal programmes in areas that fall under exclusive provincial jurisdiction. Following the failed referendum of 1995, which proposed a new relationship between Québec and the rest of Canada, the central government launched a series of initiatives in the fields of education, healthcare and, more recently, municipal politics, to make its presence felt in those provincial sectors.[18]

Québec provincial parties of various stripes, from Jean Charest's Liberals (federalists), to Mario Dumont's Adéquistes (autonomists) to Bernard Landry's Péquistes (autonomists/secessionists), have all denounced the central government's intrusion into areas of provincial policy. Others, like Claude Ryan, a former leader of the Québec Liberal Party, argue that federal–provincial negotiations have too often failed due to unnecessary inflexibility on the part of the central government. Ryan stated:

> This vision contains an abstract and doctrinaire equality of individuals and provinces; it denies any form of asymmetry in our federal system. This vision was at the root of the failure of the Meech Lake Accord. It was also present in discussions leading to the Framework Agreement [Canada's Social Union, 1999–2002]. Similar causes usually produce similar effects; no serious progress will ever be realized with Quebec as long as this vision prevails.[19]

Therefore, to borrow Ronald Watts' terminology, is there in Canada "a supportive federal culture" that can help to ease the tensions between constitutive minority nations? Despite the tensions in Québec–Canada relations, Watts remains confident. If "past Canadian experience confirms the importance of such a political culture",[20] the central government's present practices tip the scales in favour of a strong centralizing trend.[21] In Québec, the Séguin Commission on fiscal imbalance has clearly demonstrated the extent to which Ottawa takes advantage of its dominant position, forcing member states to toe its line[22] or else money will not be available for their own programmes and taxpayers will run the risk of paying twice for the same service.

Rather than pushing an imperialist agenda,[23] it seems more appropriate to seek a balance between self-rule and shared rule so that political institutions reflect Canada's societal make-up and are more in tune with a covenant tradition.

Ernest Renan's daily plebiscite

A third body of literature pertaining to the management of diversity in multinational federations centres around Ernest Renan's work. Renan coined the term "daily plebiscite" to portray the extent to which people need to be informed, consulted and involved in the development of state policies. This notion paves the way towards democratic deliberation and constitutes a genuine commitment to an open process of negotiation for members of a federation built on multiple national groupings. In short, it involves empowerment through the potential for resistance.[24]

James Tully's theoretical work is highly relevant here because he updates Renan's depiction of a political contract by trying to identify ways of recognizing national diversity in complex political settings. Tully believes that it is essential for political activities to be inter-subjective, continuous, agonic as well as multi-logical. In other words, the process of negotiation among member states has to be open, that is, an "activity-oriented" process rather than an "end-state" process where all is fixed and power relations are predetermined.[25] As with Renan's portrayal, peoples here are free to deliberate and to decide their own future.

Examining the Supreme Court of Canada's 28 August 1998 Reference Re the Secession of Quebec, Tully concludes that it describes an open process for negotiation which attenuates the perception, derived from the written text, of the Constitution Act 1982 as a straitjacket.[26] Tully is of the view that Canada, as

> a multinational democracy is free and legitimate, therefore, when its constitution treats the constituent nations as peoples with the right to self-determination in some appropriate constitutional form, such as the right to initiate constitutional change. This enables them to engage freely in negotiations of reciprocal disclosure and acknowledgement as they develop and amend their modes of recognition and cooperation, in conjunction with the fair reconciliation of other forms of diversity.[27]

In (multinational) federations, state stakeholders are sometimes associated with a central government that sees itself as the only legitimate political actor. This undermines the legitimacy of federal practices and requires our attention. The danger is that the central government may be viewed as the only government that matters, leading to what Ernest Renan described in *Qu'est-ce qu'une nation* as "one state, one culture".

In multinational federations, the principle of divisible sovereignty[28] gains some ascendancy since it is conceivable that internal nations, such as national communities like Scotland, Catalonia and Québec, should be able to exercise increased powers almost as if they were quasi-independent states. Rainer Bauböck goes further when he argues that the concept of multinational federation "rejects the conservative realist approach that views claims to self-government rights of national minorities as a threat to the territorial integrity of existing states".[29] In a globalizing world, this scenario gains support in countries where national boundaries coincide with the borders of the states in the federation, since the nearest government is often viewed as the one where citizens can exercise the strongest influence.

In addition, debates surrounding theoretical pressures in favour of multinational federations also imply that culture matters and that it is essential to find ways for institutions to reflect deep societal diversity. For national and sub-national minorities, it is

> a societal culture – that is, a culture which provides its members with meaningful ways of life across the full range of human activities, including social, educational, religious, recreational, and economic life, encompassing both public and private spheres. These cultures tend to be territorially concentrated, and based on a shared language. [...]
>
> [...] for a culture to survive and develop in the modern world, given the pressures towards the creation of a single common culture in each country, it must be a societal culture. Given the enormous significance of social institutions in our lives, and in determining our options, any culture which is not a societal culture will be reduced to ever-decreasing marginalization.[30]

Clearly, "national cultures" have an advantage to the extent that they reflect the values of the dominant political community in a (multi) national federal setting. The notion of "global society" has been utilized to depict the extent to which Québec, as a region state, is highly cohesive. It is global in the sense that it already constitutes a host society in its own right, possesses strong liberal corporate structures in which government, business and labour work together, and has high international visibility.[31]

Creative politics: healthy tensions and unresolved issues

The prevailing views in the literature suggest that there are many contending issues to be reckoned with and that further theoretical work is necessary. One thing that is sure, however, is that authors such as Rawls, Elazar and Renan have their followers. The objective to be pursued now is not to argue that one author is right while the other two are wrong, but rather to assess the extent to which their influential work has helped to reveal healthy tensions with respect to the Westphalian model and take into account the many unresolved issues in democratic federations.

For instance, Elazar warns us against an excessive desire to centralize power and stresses the need to find an appropriate balance between self-rule and shared rule, inviting public officials to be more inventive and open to a variety of models that can accommodate national communities. This position is even more powerful at a time when, to use the phraseology of David Held, "All independent states may retain a legal claim to 'effective supremacy over what occurs within their territories,' but this is significantly compromised by the growing enmeshment of 'the national' with transnational influences."[32]

Rawls' work has often been used (frequently for the wrong reasons) to discredit any serious questioning of dominant relationships within regimes. Experts have often wrapped themselves in the "veil" of Rawls' procedural liberalism to deny national minorities their right to self-determination.[33] The most common argument is based on the idea that it would be too risky for countries to be founded on the principle of justice because that could lead to political instability by making it more difficult to reach compromises among national communities. This can be seen in the Government of Canada's decision to circumvent the federal Reference Re. the Secession of Québec and adopt Bill C-20 on clarity (see Chapter 5). By changing the rules to its own advantage, in the name of Canada's political and economic stability, the Government of Canada sought to bypass the Reference's conclusions, which would have made it possible for Québec to democratically pursue its goal of national recognition.

Thus, the notion of a cooperative scheme in perpetuity has been presented as a justification for non-recognition of (sub-)national claims, in the name of an overarching, sometimes smothering majority nationalism, thereby helping to eliminate the possibility that a national minority could, in accordance with Kymlicka's argument, guarantee "its ability to make decisions in certain areas without being outvoted by the larger society".[34]

With the creation of several new nation-states since the late 1980s, it has become clear that we must develop models that can further accommodate national minorities by legitimating new institutions. Otherwise secession may become one of the only avenues available in democratic societies. The Westphalian model needs to be revamped, and one way of doing so is by giving proper exposure to the concept of multinational federalism.[35]

The value of the concept of multinational federalism becomes clear when we consider its added potential to improve our democratic practices. As we have noted in this book, and in keeping with Reg Whitaker's point of view,[36] while federalism provides a more refined definition of sovereignty, the notion of multinational federalism gives meaning to federal conceptions of citizenship. The establishment of multinational federalism as an ideal type is a step towards bringing more diverse societies into the political equation. This is vital, for national minorities are experiencing a feeling of alienation because power appears to be escaping them through a process of globalization which, in turn, is accompanied by a further quest for centralization on the part of existing states.

Multinational federalism allows us to expand our notion of citizenship and possibly develop a theory of genuinely differentiated citizenship. In the Canadian context, debates between proceduralists and communitarians with respect to Québec's right of secession, as well as Aboriginal claims to self-government, have enriched political attitudes and helped to legitimize both liberal currents of thought.

Such debates have also led liberals to consider new institutions that reflect "deep diversity"[37] in pluralist democratic societies. With a view to avoiding a secessionist trajectory, multinational federalism constitutes a way forward and should be considered as having healing potential for communities that share many values, though perhaps not the same cultural, political and sociological profiles. In other words, what is wrong with the emergence of multinational federalism if the societal projects pursued by member states are founded on liberal premises?

Obviously, power alone should not dictate how multinational federalism operates. That would result in disrespectful and anti-democratic majority nationalism. This is the very essence of the problem, leading national minorities either to ask for a reworking of the way the existing state operates or to affirm their right to secede.

Indeed, Michael Ignatieff, a former proponent of cosmopolitanism, reminds us with regard to Québec–Canada relations that,

At the moment, might lies with the majority and right with the minority. Mutual recognition must rebalance the relationship, with both power and legitimacy finding a new equilibrium. Then, and only then, will we be able to live together in peace in two countries at once, a community of rights-bearing equals and a community of self-governing nations.[38]

To get there, we need a feeling of trust and respect for the Constitution of the type that can be found in the Supreme Court of Canada's Reference Re. the Secession of Quebec. In their decision, the nine chief justices establish four principles on the basis of which it is possible to negotiate in a federal setting such as Canada: a democratic tradition, federal practices, constitutionalism and the rule of law, and respect for minority rights. If there is compliance with these principles, Québec can freely enter into negotiation with Canada in order to be recognized on its own terms. In sum, mutual respect on the part of the communities involved and a sense of constitutional morality are necessary if negotiations are to be worthy of the name.[39]

Conclusion

> We cannot erase collective problems by talking about them too much;
> they remain because we have not resolved them. Never giving in to
> weariness and obstinately bringing them back into the public arena
> seem to be the duties of those who have not abandoned thought.[1]

Study of Canada's situation, particularly in light of European experiences, shows that federalism is a key tool for facilitating the management of community conflicts. Since it is more sensitive to the community claims of different nations living together, multinational federalism makes it possible to establish a more progressive model of governance with greater potential for allowing government officials to meet the expectations of national communities in terms of representation, equity and justice. The stability of current political regimes is at stake.

In this book, we have reviewed the primary advances made in recent years in the area of comparative federalism[2] and, at the same time, taken into account the too-often neglected right of minority nations to full recognition in existing states. Canadian–Québec dynamics have been at the heart of our study and we have used the example to assess the experiences of national minorities in Spain, Belgium and the United Kingdom to identify avenues for improvement in the long term.

One of the greatest advantages of federalism in a world that is sometimes hostile to national diversity within countries is that it enables different political communities to exercise certain powers in order to facilitate their political emancipation. We have seen in the case of Canada that central government officials are uncomfortable with Québec's desire for national affirmation. The same applies with respect to Aboriginal nations in Canada. Sometimes power relations

favour the political centre to such an extent that other political entities come to wish for independence. In a way, this is a failure of federalism to achieve its full potential. This failure poses problems
because, in some so-called federal states, instead of sharing sovereignty, the central government imposes its authority on members of
the federation, even when the constitution does not give it full power
in certain areas of jurisdiction, as is the case with healthcare, education and transportation in Canada, which are under the exclusive
jurisdiction of the member states of the federation.

The purpose of multinational federalism should be obvious to
anyone who believes in furthering democratic practices in liberal
democratic states. It helps bring power closer to citizens and invites
majority nations to show solidarity towards minorities while continuing their political associations. Multinational federalism is a promising avenue for contemporary states specifically because it leads to
refinement of democratic practices in the same way that, according to
Stuart Hall, the identity policy

> works with and through difference, which is able to build those
> forms of solidarity and identification which make common strug-
> gle and resistance possible but without suppressing the real het-
> erogeneity of interests and identities, and which can effectively
> draw the political boundary lines without which political contes-
> tation is impossible, without fixing those boundaries for
> eternity.[3]

The establishment of multinational federalism is a major step
forward for diversity management in that it initiates promising
debate on recognition, helps pinpoint defining moments as poten-
tially empowering or constraining, and compensates for inadequate
recognition by revisiting original compacts.

We need to study multinational federalism in greater detail[4] as a
complement to studies focusing specifically on federalism as a tool
for enfranchising minority nations in complex democratic states. In
sum, and to quote Mitchell Cohen, it is best to think about the future
of minority nations by focusing on "rooted cosmopolitanism, which
accepts a multiplicity of roots and branches and which rests on the
legitimacy of plural loyalties, of standing in many circles, but with
common ground".[5]

The national diversity that characterizes most contemporary states
will not diminish; we must, therefore, envision means of writing it
into political institutions, otherwise the world around us will become

increasingly uncertain and we will see the rise of political undertakings that are less and less respectful of societal cultures and more inclined towards coercion. Like Tzvetan Todorov, we believe it is urgent to return to the spirit of the Enlightenment. Todorov reminds us that "[i]t is in multiplicity, which we might have believed was a handicap, that the thinkers of the Enlightenment saw the advantage of Europe [...] and how plurality could give birth to unity".[6] Todorov then notes that in the case of China, vast potential has been "smothered by the existence of an immense unified empire, where the unchallenged reign of authority, traditions and established reputations has caused thinking to stagnate".[7]

The message could not be clearer: it must be possible for diversity to be fully expressed. At the same time, individuals, groups, communities and nations need open, creative futures before them. It is important to establish appropriate political avenues so that national diversity and political unity can co-exist.[8] In sum, given a choice between Trudeau and his model of mechanical federalism,[9] in which all citizens are equal and have the same relationship with the central government, and Charles Taylor, who describes a philosophical position open to multinational diversity, enabling members of different national communities to fully express themselves (see Chapter 3), advanced liberal democracies should choose the latter. Showing this is the challenge that this book has tried to meet by offering a humanist reading of community relations in multinational democratic states.

In short, if countries characterized by national diversity manage to establish federal traditions based on community rights and agree to share sovereignty, we will enter a new, promising era for coming generations. Perhaps "might" will no longer automatically "make right". The tragic events that have marked many contemporary states, such as Cyprus, Iraq, Yugoslavia, Georgia and Sri Lanka, require that we take multinational federalism seriously and that we distance ourselves from standardizing models that have too often been imposed on minority nations since the beginning of Westphalian times. Todorov reminds us that it is specifically

> [t]he ability to integrate differences without making them disappear [that] distinguishes Europe from other major political groupings in the world. [...] Europe recognizes not only the rights of individuals but also those of the historical, cultural and political communities that constitute the Union's member states.[10]

In fact, Todorov errs by not taking his thought further and including the historical nations at the origin of modern European states in his analysis. In that, he follows the Westphalian tradition. However, it is a step that we must not hesitate to take to ensure the sustainability of democratic political regimes.

As the epigraph from Fernand Dumont at the beginning of the Conclusion reminds us, much determination is required on the part of political players to find solutions to the collective challenges facing modern nations. However, for that, we first have to agree to debate the merits of the theses advanced by the various stakeholders. Respect and reflection must permeate the foundations of truly democratic debate so that minority nations are not required to take shapes that are foreign to them or obliged to give up offering their constituents societal plans that promise freedom and justice. This kind of openness can guarantee healthy democracy and solidarity among peoples on a planetary scale.

At a time when many countries in crisis around the world are favouring federal schemes, we have to wonder why countries such as Canada and Spain are abandoning or beginning to lose trust in them. In this book, we have shown that Canadians are gradually forsaking federal practices and adopting a national identity that is increasingly hostile to deep diversity, thereby alienating the Québécois and First Nations from central institutions. In Spain, leading stakeholders have come to interpret federalism as weakening the central government. We believe this is a mistake and that federalism should instead be seen as a system that strengthens democratic practices.[11] Today, these two countries are facing huge challenges that they will only be able to surmount if the majority nations demonstrate openness to the minority nations. In Canada, the election of the Conservatives under the leadership of Stephen Harper in January 2006 brought hope back to many Québécois, who support the ideas underlying the federalism of openness that Harper invoked during the election campaign. It is still too early to measure the real impact of the change in attitude in terms of Québécois trust in central institutions. However, for now, it is the only avenue that is even slightly open and sensitive to Québécois demands. Will the federalism of openness proposed by Stephen Harper's Conservatives suffice to shore up the shaky legitimacy of federal institutions in the eyes of minority nations? Nothing could be less certain. It is unlikely that the Québécois will be satisfied by another political programme inspired by procedural liberalism and insensitive to the societal cultures and values underlying communitarian liberalism.

Notes

Introduction: the merits of federalism and new awareness of the multination

1 Zapata-Barrero, 2004.
2 Stepan, 1999, p. 19.
3 King, 1982.
4 Livingston, 1952, pp. 81–95.
5 To assess the two traditions, see the chapters by Chevrier, Karmis and Laforest in A.-G. Gagnon, ed., 2006.
6 I am borrowing this description from Campuzano Carvajal, ed., 2001.
7 Leton and Miroir, 1999, pp. 7–71.
8 Leroy, 1996.
9 Note the work by J. Tully; for example, Tully, 1999, pp. 13–36.
10 Loughlin, 2007.
11 Tully, 1999, p. 30 [our translation].
12 Smiley, 1987, p. 9.
13 See Karmis and Norman, 2005, pp. 3–21.
14 Trudeau, 1968, p. 150. While his many years at the head of the government were sometimes problematic concerning respect for the rights of the First Nations and the Québec nation, Pierre Trudeau nonetheless raised the political class' awareness of federalism's usefulness as a foundation for managing disputes.
15 See Trujillo, 1967, pp. 136–137.
16 By "Carlism", we are referring to the desire to re-establish the Ancien régime and the independence of the Basque and Navarre areas.
17 Trujillo, 1967, p. 127; Molas, 1966, pp. 21–24.
18 Molas, 1966, pp. 144–153.
19 Cascajo Castro, 1993, pp. 17–20. There are different opinions about the real characteristics of integral federalism. See work by the following for further information: F. Thomas Y Valiente, P. Gonzalez Casanova, S. Albornoz, M.B. Garcia Alvarez and F. Sesgado.

1 Memory and national identity in Catalonia and Québec

1 The first version of this chapter was presented at the Québec–Catalogne day organized by the Centre d'Estudis de Temes Contemporanis at Bar-

celona on 8 June 2006. I would like to thank in particular Albert Balcells i Gonzalez, Louis Balthazar, Jacques Beauchemin, Jordi Casassas Ymbert, Marc Duenas, Agusti Nicolau Coll and Marc Leprêtre for their valuable comments on the first version.

2 Taylor, 1993b, p. 46.
3 Taylor, 1993b, p. 52.
4 Taylor, 1994a, pp. 42–99.
5 Taylor, 1994b, p. 25.
6 In writings on nationalism, there are arguments against this proposition, some of which go so far as to suggest that this form of assertion of identity is antithetical to Enlightenment liberal values. However, Yael Tamir and several other authors have since shown that liberalism and nationalism co-exist harmoniously in a number of contemporary states. See Tamir, 1993.
7 See Giner, ed., 1998.
8 Dumont, 1993, p. 236 [our translation].
9 There is a general consensus that the poet Aribau is the father of the movement, with his 1833 work entitled *La Oda a la Patrià*.
10 Taylor, 1993b, p. 56.
11 Anderson, 1996.
12 For an analysis on the notion of reference points for identity, see Maclure and Gagnon, eds, 2001.
13 Cf. Todorov, 2002, especially Chapter 6 entitled "La barque humaniste", pp. 209–248, in which the author says that we have to think universally but at the same time strengthen diversity.
14 Dumont, 1993, p. 219 [our translation]. Referring to Catalonia, Michael Keating says,

> So Catalan civil society remains a bastion of Catalan values and identity and an important arena for nation-building. Like the Catalan political arena, it reflects the multiple identity of most Catalans, linking the local, the Spanish and, increasingly, the European and international arenas.
>
> (2001a, p. 183)

15 Turgeon, 1999, pp. 35–56.
16 Vilar, 1947, p. 70 [our translation].
17 Jenson was the first to point out that there is a dual-citizenship regime in Canada. See Jenson, 1998, pp. 215–239.
18 Gagnon, 2000a, p. A-7.
19 Langlois, 1991, pp. 95–108.
20 For a better understanding of issues concerning immigration in Catalonia and Québec, see Zapata-Barrero, 2004 and Aubarell *et al.*, eds, 2004.
21 See Balcells, 1991.
22 Belliveau, 2002, p. 33 [our translation].
23 See Vilar, 1977.
24 Carrasco, cited in Belliveau, 2002, p. 30 [our translation].
25 J. Belliveau, 2002, p. 34 [our translation].
26 See Guerena, 2001, p. 24 [our translation].
27 According to A. Balcells at the Québec–Catalonia day organized by the Centre d'Estudis de Temes Contemporanis in Barcelona on 8 June 2006.

28 This date is even more important because it corresponds with the beginning of the period of standardization of the Catalan language, which facilitated the emergence of the Catalan identity as we know it today.

29 For a concise study of the Mancommunitat, see Balcells Gonzalez *et al.*, 1996.

30 King Juan Carlos' 16 February 1976 speech can be found in Sánchez-Terán, 1988, pp. 49 ff.

31 "El Estado se organiza teritorialmente en municipios, en provincias y en las Communidades Autonomas que se constituyan."

32 Miguel Herrero de Minon, who was one of the members of the constitutional commission that led to the establishment of the Spanish state of autonomies, makes major distinctions between historical communities and autonomous communities in general. See Herrero de Minon, 1995.

33 Campuzano Carvajal, 2001, p. 162 [our translation].

34 Section 2 of the 1978 Constitution:

> The Constitution is based on the indissoluble unity of the Spanish Nation, the common and indivisible homeland of all Spaniards; it recognizes and guarantees the right to self-government of the nationalities and regions of which it is composed and the solidarity among them all.

35 See Wynn, 1990, p. 223.

36 For an in-depth study of the bijural system in Canada, see Gaudreault-Desbiens, 2006.

37 For further details, see Gagnon and Turgeon, 2003, pp. 1–23.

38 Neatby, 1972, p. 1.

39 Lahaise and Vallerand, 1999.

40 Tully, 1995b.

41 As an illustration, see work by C. Bariteau, such as "L'Acte de Québec (1774), assise de l'*Indirect rule* toujours d'actualité" (2000).

42 Bouchard, 2000, p. 96 [our translation].

43 Laforest, 1992, p. 254.

44 Dumont, 1995, pp. 31–48 (Chapter 2: "La fin d'un malentendu historique").

45 For further details on this period, see Gagnon and Iacovino, 2007, especially Chapter 2, pp. 28–32.

46 Cited in Arès, 1967, pp. 61–62 [our translation].

47 See below (page 41) for a more in-depth discussion of the three principles.

48 The Government of Québec established a national commission to raise Québécois' awareness of the idea of establishing a properly Québécois citizenship. See Commission des États généraux sur la situation et l'avenir de la langue française au Québec (Larose Commission), 2001.

49 See Gagnon, 2003a, p. 153 for a longer discussion.

50 See Gagnon, 1998, p. 170.

51 Balcells, 1991, pp. 45 ff.

52 Nunez Seixas, 1999, p. 54 and ff.

53 Moreno, 2001; Requejo, 2005.

54 Tully, 1999, p. 16 [our translation].

55 Tully, 1999, p. 15 [our translation].
56 Tully, 1999, p. 14 [our translation].
57 MacCormick, cited in Nootens, 2004, p. 52 [our translation].
58 Karmis, 2003, p. 92 [our translation].
59 I am borrowing the very evocative title of the work by A. Dieckhoff, *La constellation des appartenances. Nationalisme, libéralisme et pluralisme* (2004).
60 Castells, 1999, especially pp. 47–70.
61 See Maclure, 2001, p. 262 [our translation]. For an excellent study on the heterogeneity of cultural identities among post-colonial authors and specialists of federalism, see Maclure and Karmis, 2001, pp. 361–385.
62 Campuzano Carajal, 2001, p. 163 [our translation].
63 See Keating, 1997, pp. 145–157.
64 See the work by D. Miller, especially Chapter 5, "Nationality in Decline", in *On Nationality*, 1995, pp. 155–182.
65 Miller, 1995, p. 173.
66 Gagné and Langlois, 2006, pp. 440–456.
67 Ferry, 1998, pp. 205–206, cited in Dieckhoff, 2004, pp. 30–31 [our translation].
68 Tully, 1995b, p. 30.
69 For a discussion of the Catalan nation, see the very interesting work by Guibernau, 2002; and for a study of the Québec nation, see Venne, ed., 2000.
70 See Chapter 6 for a development of Ernest Renan's ideas.
71 Government of Québec, *Conseil des communautés culturelles et de l'immigration* 1993, p. 11 [our translation].
72 See the work by Keating, including *Les défis du nationalisme moderne. Québec, Catalogne, Écosse*, 1997.
73 See Kymlicka, 2001.

2 The normative foundations of asymmetrical federalism: the Canadian situation from a comparative perspective

1 This chapter develops an argument that I initially put forth in *Multinational Democracies* (Cambridge: Cambridge University Press, 2001), and that has been improved by comments from many colleagues, including Rainer Bauböck, Raffaele Iacovino, Dimitrios Karmis, Guy Laforest, François Rocher and James Tully.
2 In the literature on comparative federalism, the first author to identify the importance of this factor was W.S. Livingston. See Livingston, 1952, pp. 81–95.
3 McRae, 1979b, pp. 675–688.
4 Rabushka and Shepsle, 1971, p. 462.
5 Lijphart, 1968; see also Lijphart, 1982, pp. 166–186.
6 McRae, 1983, 1986.
7 Kukathas, 1992, pp. 105–139, reprinted in Kymlicka, ed., 1995c, p. 231. Note the influence of J. Rawls. See *A Theory of Justice*, 1972.
8 Taylor, 1993b, pp. 181–184.
9 For further information, see Watts, 2002. See also de Villiers, ed., 1994.
10 See Jouve and Gagnon, eds, 2006.

11 Linz, 1997, pp. 13–20.

12 For a development of this point, see Gagnon, 2006.

13 Requejo, 1999, p. 270. For an analogous and complementary development, see also Maiz and Requejo, eds, 2005.

14 King, 1982.

15 For a more in-depth analysis of de facto and de jure allocation of power, see Gagnon and Garcea, 1988, pp. 304–325.

16 See Gagnon and Montcalm, 1992.

17 Milne, 1991, pp. 285–307.

18 For a study of the attempted constitutional reform, see Bariteau *et al.*, 1992.

19 Citizen's Forum on Canada's Future, 1991, p. 124.

20 Citizen's Forum on Canada's Future, 1991, p. 140.

21 Kymlicka, 1998b, pp. 111–150; Kymlicka and Raviot, 1997, p. 791.

22 Whitaker, 1993, pp. 107–114.

23 The partisan dynamic during the referendum on a new political status for Catalonia in Spain completely changed between September 2005 and March 2006, from solidarity in action to a heated struggle between political groups with a view to the next election.

24 For an illustration of this, see Bakvis and Skogstad, 2002.

25 Here, we are partly in debt to one of the most illustrious communitarian philosophers – see Sandel, 1989.

26 Ketcham, ed., 1986.

27 LaSelva, 1996, pp. 38 and 41.

28 Vipond, 1995, p. 102.

29 Arès, 1967.

30 The Tremblay report ordered by the Government of Québec in 1953 was the first official document to clearly formulate the role of the Québec Government concerning its own responsibilities. See Bouchard, 2000.

31 Dumont, 1995, p. 54.

32 Tully, 1995b, pp. 116–139.

33 Referring to the patriation of the Canadian constitution from Great Britain in 1981–1982, Tully notes that none of the three conventions were respected. See Tully, 1999, pp. 13–36.

34 For a more in-depth explanation of this topic, see de Villiers, 1995. See also Kymlicka and Raviot, 1997, pp. 779–843. The latter is an essay summarizing a series of articles presented at conferences held at Laval University and the University of British Columbia on 30 September to 2 October 1996 on the theme "Living Together in Federal States: International Aspects of Federalism".

35 Cairns, 1991, p. 88.

36 Fossas, 1999, pp. 275–301.

37 Vernon, 1988, p. 10.

38 Whitaker, 1992, p. 167.

39 See Lacasta-Zabalda, 1998.

40 Tully, 1992, pp. 77–96. Scottist jurist Stephen Tierney investigates in greater detail the avenue opened by James Tully. See, for example, *Constitutional Law and National Pluralism*, 2004.

41 For a discussion of the importance of making an additional distinction between national and collective rights, see Requejo, 1999, pp. 255–286.

Note that with respect to Canada, a study by Avigail Eisenberg shows that the justices of the Supreme Court of Canada take collective rights into account in their decisions. See Eisenberg, 1994, pp. 3–21.

42 For a discussion of various complex expressions of egality, see Castineira, 1999, pp. 111–114.

43 Lenihan *et al.*, 1994, p. 166.

44 Burelle, 1995, p. 105.

45 Tully, 1994a, pp. 157–178.

46 Laforest, 1992, pp. 183, 185.

47 This type of argument, though at the level of the state of autonomies in Spain, was upheld by both the defenders and opponents of a new status for Catalonia in Spain in spring 2006.

48 Spinner, 1994, p. 154.

49 Montesquieu [1849], p. 316.

50 Montesquieu [1849].

51 It is interesting to note that the same argument was recently advanced by political economists Enrico Sparaole and Alberto Alesina in *The Size of Nations*, 2003. According to Sparaole and Alesina, the size of nations is the result of a trade-off between the benefits of size (economy of scale) and the costs engendered by the need to govern heterogeneity (diversity) of preferences in a large nation. In sum, a small nation is able to respond more easily and more "democratically" to the demands of its population, while a large nation is able to meet its citizens' needs at a lower cost because it has a larger pool of taxpayers.

52 Proudhon, 1979, pp. 43–49.

53 Webber, 1994, p. 204.

54 In light of this observation, it is difficult to believe that a serene dialogue can be established between standardizing Canadians and differenciating Québécois. The same dynamic applies in many other cases, such as in relations between historical nations and representatives of the Spanish government.

55 Requejo, 1999, pp. 260–261.

56 Taylor, 1993b, pp. 181–184.

57 Taylor, 1993b, p. 100.

58 Some authors from English Canada have suggested removing Québec's status as a province to solve the problems arising from asymmetry with respect to the principle of provincial equality (see Cairns, 1991, p. 89). Others have noted that Québec, in concert with other member states of the federation, could obtain significant new powers tailored to its needs by embedding the concept of competition, which would make the provinces predominant (see Milne, 1991, p. 302). Normatively, in the former scenario, Québec would be recognized as a distinct political community, while in the latter it would have to be considered as simply one of the components of a decentralized Canada.

59 Fossas, 1999, pp. 275–301.

60 Ajzenstat, 1995, p. 127.

61 Ajzenstat, 1995, p. 127.

62 Beauchemin, 2004.

63 See Pal, 1993.

64 According to Ajzenstat (1995, p. 132), in Canada,

The quarrel is not really about the requirements that will satisfy justice. It is about what justice *is*. To be treated justly now means being first in a constitutional pecking order, and each group advances the definition of justice – that is, the scheme of ranking – that gives it pre-eminence.

65   LaSelva, 1996, p. 171.
66   Gagnon, 1993, pp. 15–44; Smith, 1995, p. 16.
67   Kymlicka raises a related point: "What is clear, I think, is that if there is a viable way to promote a sense of solidarity and common purpose in a multination state, it will involve accommodating, rather than subordinating, national identities" (Kymlicka, 1995a, p. 189).
68   For a discussion of the notion of indetermination of the political process in Spain, see Maiz, 2005, pp. 18–23.
69   See Delpérée, 1995, p. 13 [our translation].
70   McRoberts' work provides a clear picture of the events that led to Québec's isolation in the Canadian political family. See *Un pays à refaire: l'échec des politiques constitutionnelles canadiennes*, 1999. See also Tully, 1999, pp. 13–36.

3   The emerging phenomenon of the multination

1   An initial version of this chapter was presented at the international colloquium on "Ces liens qui unissent. Gérer la diversité au Canada et dans l'Union Européenne", organized by the Réseau européen d'études canadiennes, Brussels, Université Libre de Bruxelles, 17–19 November 2005. Comments from Francisco Colom-Gonzalez, John Erik Fossum, Jane Jenson, Geneviève Nootens, Johanne Poirier and Philip Van Parijs were greatly appreciated.
2   See Rawls, 1972, and his most complete work, *Political Liberalism*, 1993. See also Chapter 6 for a discussion of Rawls' legacy.
3   Young, 1990; Gutmann, 2003; Yuval-Davis, 1997, pp. 1–25.
4   According to R. Dworkin, a society is liberal so long as it adopts no substantive approach to goals pursued in life; only procedural laws should be taken into consideration.
5   Taylor, 1993a, p. 92.
6   See McRae, 1979a, pp. 69–82 and Lijphart, 1977, p. 25, in which the author identifies four major "consociational" principles that we call here "consensual democracy". See Chapter 1 for a complementary discussion.
7   Smith, 1985, pp. 1–68. For a more detailed discussion, see Bickerton *et al.*, 2002.
8   Meisel and Rocher, eds, 1999.
9   See Gagnon and Latouche, 1991.
10   For a detailed discussion of the Trudeau years, see Bickerton *et al.*, 2003, pp. 129–157 (Chapter 5: "Le libéralisme universaliste de Pierre Trudeau").
11   See the discussion on international relations in Chapter 5.
12   A. Eisenberg has clearly shown that the Charter can protect both individual and collective rights when groups claiming rights are spread across Canada. See Eisenberg, 1994, pp. 3–21.

13 Taylor, 1993a, p. 94.

14 See, among others, Venne, ed., 2000.

15 See the special volume of *Scottish Affairs* (MacInnes and McCrone, eds, 2001) and Aubarell *et al.*, eds, 2004.

16 See Rioux, 2000, in which the author reviews this phenomenon in numerous national communities, including Catalonia, Scotland, Slovenia, the Basque country, Ireland, Wallonia, Flanders, Slovakia and the Navaho Indian community.

17 Some analysts will object and say that Québec might be satisfied by Stephen Harper's Conservative government, which came to power in January 2006 with the promise to create "open federalism" giving each member state of the federation greater room to manoeuvre. However, events of the past three years have cast a shadow on the plan, which initially won the support of part of the Québec electorate. The enthusiasm engendered by "open federalism" won seats for ten members of Parliament out of a possible 75 in the election of January 2006.

18 Taylor, 1993a, pp. 94–95.

19 See, among others, Tully, 2000.

20 Pierré-Caps, 1995, pp. 265–266 [our translation]. The uprisings in French suburbs in fall 2005 confirm that a condition in which power is assumed without being shared can only last for so long.

21 For work done by members of the GRSP, see www.creqc.uqam.ca/grsp/grsp.html.

22 Resnick, 1994b, p. 71.

23 On the federal principle, see Burelle, 1996. See also Noël, 1998, pp. 263–295.

24 On treaty federalism, see White, 2002, pp. 89–114; Papillon, 2006, pp. 461–485.

25 See Gagnon and Latouche, 1991, pp. 23–90, for a longer discussion.

26 Gagnon, 2003a, pp. 151–174.

27 See Seymour, 1999, for an enlightening theoretical discussion of inter-community relations in Québec; see especially Chapters 11 to 13.

28 Pierré-Caps, 1995.

29 This idea is applied to the case of Spain in Maiz, 2005.

30 See Keating, 2001b, pp. 19–20, in which Keating proposes distinguishing multinationalism (i.e. several national communities living in a single state) from plurinationalism (i.e. numerous national identities that can describe different citizens).

31 See Meadwell, 2003, pp. 219–238; Jedwab, 2004.

32 Resnick, 1994a, p. 7.

33 Gagnon and Laforest, 1993, pp. 470–491; McRoberts, 1999; Tully, 2001, pp. 1–33.

34 See Chapter 6, "Le libéralisme communautarien de C. Taylor", and Chapter 7, "Le libéralisme universaliste de Pierre Trudeau", in Bickerton *et al.*, eds, 2003, pp. 99–128 and 129–157.

35 Bickerton *et al.*, 2006, p. 139. Moreover, Trudeau was a great defender of Canadian identity in relation to the United States. Ironically, while he opposed Québec nationalism, he was the herald of Canadian nationalism.

36 *Delgamuukw* v. *British Columbia* (1997) 3 S.C.R. 1010.

37 In light of the distressing recent events at Kashechewan, where 1200 of the 1700 residents on the reserve had to be evacuated at the end of October 2005 because the water was contaminated, we have to wonder when Aboriginal people will have the right to live in dignity on their own land.
38 See C. Taylor's influential text, "Atomism", 1985, pp. 187–210.
39 See Rupnik, 1995.
40 Trudeau, 1968, p. 193.
41 See Laforest, 1992.
42 Cairns, 1991, p. 80. For a more detailed discussion of how the Charter weakens federalism in Canada, see Chapter 5.
43 See J. Tully's very enlightening text, "Le fédéralisme à voies multiples et la Charte", 1994b, p. 128.
44 Tully, 1994c, p. 180.
45 Tully, 1994c, p. 183.
46 This quotation from John Holmes, which dates from when he was the Director General of the Canadian Institute of International affairs, is taken from Russell, 1966, p. 369.
47 See the GRSP site: www.creqc.uqam.ca/grsp/grsp.html.
48 See, among others, Gagnon and Tully, eds, 2001 and Gagnon *et al.*, eds, 2003.
49 Ignatieff, 2001, p. 120.
50 Flanagan, 2000. Flanagan is one of the intellectuals who have influenced the political path of the current Prime Minister of Canada, Stephen Harper. This might partly explain the central government's about-face, and its refusal today to implement the Kelowna Accord that was signed by Paul Martin's Liberal government and the First Nations a few months before the 2006 federal election.
51 Cairns, 2000.
52 Tully, 1994c, p. 180.
53 Harty and Murphy, 2005.
54 Kernerman, 2005.
55 In a text full of foresight, J. Tully comes to the conclusion that Québec is not free in the Canadian federation. See Tully, 1999, pp. 13–36.

4 Executive federalism and the exercise of democracy in Canada

1 An initial version of this text was presented at the International Workshop on Federalism and Democracy organized by the Centre for Federal Studies, University of Kent, Canterbury, England, 2–6 April 2006. Comments from Michael Burgess, Paolo Dardanelli, Luis Moreno, Ferran Requejo and Ronald Watts were greatly appreciated. I would also like to acknowledge Charles-Antoine Sévigny's help in identifying and translating bibliographical sources and citations.
2 Fossas and Requejo, 2005; Gagnon and Tully, eds, 2001; Gagnon *et al.*, eds, 2003.
3 Weiss, 2003, pp. 293–317.
4 See Simeon and Robinson, 2004, pp. 101–126.
5 Simeon and Robinson, 1990, p. 209.
6 Whitaker, 1992, pp. 207, 206.

7   See Russell, 1993, p. 5. Russell also makes the point that the Fathers of Confederation emulated Edmund Burke more than John Locke in their approach to the Constitution (1993, p. 11).

8   Brock, 2003, pp. 70–71.

9   See Laforest, 1998, pp. 55–84. See also Gagnon and Chokri, 2005, pp. 27–28.

10   Caron *et al.*, 2006, pp. 147–182.

11   Simeon and Robinson, 1990, p. 49.

12   Simeon and Robinson, 2004, pp. 109–110. In fairness, no other western economy was capable of meeting the unprecedented challenge.

13   Brock, 2003, p. 71.

14   Smiley, 1980, p. 102.

15   Smiley, 1980, p. 91.

16   Watts, 1989, p. 4.

17   Adam, 2005, p. 2.

18   "Collaborative federalism" is also used to refer to the same thing.

19   Watts, 1989, pp. 4–5.

20   See Gagnon and Iacovino, 2007, for further information on domination by the central government.

21   Smiley, 1979, pp. 105–106.

22   Porter, 1965, p. 384.

23   Porter, 1965, p. 384.

24   Smith, 2004, p. 101.

25   Smith, 2004, p. 102.

26   Smith, 2004, p. 102.

27   Smith, 2004, pp. 102–103.

28   Smith, 2004, p. 103.

29   See Presthus, 1973.

30   Noël, 2003, p. 5. Available online at http://cpsa-acsp.ca/paper-2003/noel.pdf.

31   Brock, 1991, p. 59.

32   Reprinted in Sheppard and Valpy, 1982, p. 284.

33   See, among others, Gagnon, 1994, pp. 85–106.

34   For a discussion of Canada's Charter and its centralizing effects on governance and weakening effects on federal traditions, see Chapter 5.

35   Cairns, 1988, p. 122.

36   Simeon and Cameron, 2002, pp. 278–279.

37   Pal and Seidle, 1993, pp. 143–202.

38   For a similar interpretation, see Smith, 2002, p. 59.

39   Brock, 1995, p. 101.

40   See, among others, Pal and Seidle, 1993, pp. 143–202.

41   Lazar, 1998, pp. 3–35. See also Smith, 2002, 40–58.

42   This agreement is discussed in greater detail in Chapter 5. See also Gagnon and Iacovino, 2007, pp. 70–89.

43   See Gagnon and Segal, eds, 1999.

44   Quoted in Burelle, 2003, p. 2.

45   See Gagnon and Segal, eds, 1999. All eight analyses concurred in their interpretation and pointed in the direction of a hierarchical collaboration that was imposed by the central government without much concern for the division of powers.

46 Lazar, 2003, p. 3.
47 Adam, 2005, p. 1. In this way of understanding federalism, we can see the influence of K.C. Wheare, for whom "The federal principle requires that the general and regional governments of a country shall be independent each of the other within its sphere, shall be not subordinate one to another but co-ordinate with each other" (1967, p. 93). See also Facal, 2006, p. 241.
48 To gain a better understanding of the scope of the tension, see Lajoie, 2006, Seymour, 2006.
49 Requejo discusses this issue in *Federalisme, per a què? L'acomodacio de la diversitat en democracies plurinationals*, 1998, pp. 36–40.
50 Burelle, 2003, p. 2 [our translation]. For more on Trudeau's understanding of Canadian federalism, see Trudeau, 1991 and Burelle, 2005.
51 See Burgess and Gagnon, eds, forthcoming, which led to the April 2006 conference in Canterbury organized by the Centre for Federal Studies at Kent University.
52 Whitaker, 1992, p. 167.
53 Burgess, 2006, p. 107.
54 Cairns, 1988, p. 134.
55 Russell, 2004, p. 252.
56 Laforest, 1992; see especially Chapter 5, "Trudeau et la saga de Meech", and Chapter 7, "Allaire, Bélanger, Campeau et les propositions de renouvellement du fédéralisme". See also Laforest's more recent work (2004).
57 Noël, 2003, p. 6. A similar case can be made about weakening the federal tradition in Canada when one more closely examines the Clarity Act, enacted by Ottawa in response to Québec's desire to hold another referendum on self-determination.
58 See the discussion of the notion of nation-state in Aubarell *et al.*, 2004, pp. 95–105.
59 LaSelva, 1996, p. 25.
60 See note 46, above.
61 For a development of those principles, see Tully, 1995b.
62 During the Meech Lake debates, feminists outside of Québec argued that the distinct society clause in the proposed agreement might lead to the oppression of women in the province by facilitating repressive and discriminatory measures. Québec feminist leaders were quick to denounce this stance as reflective of ignorance. See McRoberts, 1997, pp. 199–200.
63 This theory seems to have a lot of support among economists, who argue that when it is difficult to achieve an optimal solution, it is best to fall back on the next best choice.

5 The effects of majority nationalism in Canada

1 This text completes an argument initially put forth in the context of work by the Groupe de recherche sur les sociétés plurinationales. See Gagnon, 2003b, pp. 295–312.
2 Dumont, 1995, pp. 54–55 [our translation].
3 Brubaker, 1996, p. 9.

4 Calhoun, 1997, p. 3.
5 Greenfeld, 1992, p. 488. See also her recent work, including *Nationalism and the Mind: Essays on Modern Culture*, 2006.
6 Jenson, 1993, pp. 337–358; Bashevkin, 1991.
7 Swinton and Rogerson, eds, 1988.
8 Bashevkin, 1991, p. 157.
9 See Laforest, 1998, pp. 55–84, in which he denounces the imperialistic effects of political practices prevailing in Canada.
10 Papillon and Simeon, 2004, pp. 113–140.
11 Smith, 2002, pp. 40–58; Noël, 2000, pp. 1–26.
12 Brubaker, 1996, pp. 103–104.
13 This study could very well be extended to other areas, such as labour mobility and occupational training, financial assistance for students and post-secondary education, child benefits and innovation programmes set up by the federal government in Canada.
14 See Russell, 1983a, pp. 210–238.
15 See Fortin, 2006, pp. 339–369.
16 This point is explained in detail in Gagnon, 2000b, pp. 129–154.
17 Kymlicka, 1998c.
18 Noël, 2000, pp. 1–26; see also Burelle, 1999, p. A-7.
19 For a more detailed description of the various phases of executive federalism in Canada, see Chapters 2 and 4.
20 Smith, 2002, pp. 40–58.
21 Smith, 2002, pp. 55–56.
22 This interpretation is described in detail by the Commission on the Political and Constitutional Future of Québec, in *Report of the Commission on the Political and Constitutional Future of Québec*, Québec City: Publications officielles du Québec, 1991, p. 34.
23 For an in-depth analysis of Trudeau's contribution to Canadian political culture, see Bickerton *et al.*, 2003, Chapter 7.
24 On Trudeau's use of legal nationalism against Québec nationalism, see Oliver, 1991, pp. 339–368.
25 Tully, 1995a.
26 Laforest, 1992.
27 For an analysis of the central government's role in creating the Canadian nation, see Resnick, 1994a.
28 Russell, 1983b, pp. 1–33.
29 Laforest, 1992, p. 185 [our translation].
30 Hiebert, 1996.
31 Hiebert, 1996, p. 137.
32 This argument is similar to that which increased support in the rest of Canada for the Clarity Act, which was enacted in Ottawa on 29 June 2000: "Do what you want, but we (a central, pan-Canadian institution) will have the last word!" For a discussion of this legislation, see Turp, 2000. See above (page 101) for further details on this episode.
33 Knopff and Morton, 1985, p. 149.
34 The Québec Charter of Human Rights and Freedoms is available at: www.creqc.uqam.ca.
35 Soldatos, 1988, pp. 109–123; Latouche, 1988, pp. 29–42.
36 Thérien *et al.*, 1994, pp. 259–278.

37 Balthazar, 2003, pp. 505–536. For a more in-depth study of the repercussions of the Gérin–Lajoie doctrine, see Paquin, ed., 2006.

38 The Gérin–Lajoie doctrine was mentioned for the first time on 12 April 1965 before members of the consular corps of Montréal. The complete text is available at: http://saic.gouv.qc.ca/publications/Positions/Partie2/PaulGerinLajoie1965.pdf.

39 Bastien, 1999, p. 262.

40 See Bastien, 1999, for further details.

41 Useful works on this topic include those by John Loughlin and Stéphane Paquin, respectively, *Subnational Democracy in the European Union*, 2001 and *Paradiplomatie et relations internationales. Théorie des stratégies internationales des régions face à la mondialisation*, 2004.

42 Concerning the diplomatic considerations of "Plan B", see Turp, 2000, pp. 109–145.

43 The containment policy also targeted academic circles. In 1997, senior federal officials made a number of attempts to have Canadian embassies prevent the creation of the Association internationale d'études québécoises (AIEQ). After a shaky start, during which federal public servants accused the founding members of the AIEQ of anti-patriotism, the association rallied academics in all disciplines all over the world. Today it has over 1400 members and maintains direct links with over 3000 specialists of Québec around the world.

44 Jacob, 2004, pp. 239–266.

45 See Gagnon and Tully, eds, 2001.

46 Keohane, 1984.

47 Keohane, 1984, p. 183.

48 Noël, 2000, p. 4.

49 National identity is discussed in Chapter 1.

50 Kymlicka, 1995b, p. 15.

51 Webber, 1994, p. 159.

6 Resistance and potential: the duty to consider the multination

1 This chapter expands on my discussion on diversity and identities in Québec and regions of Europe from the January 2004 colloquium at the Institut d'Études Politiques de Bordeaux. Linda Cardinal, Bernard Gagnon, Michael Keating and Jacques Palard all made very useful comments.

2 See Margalit, 1996, p. 1. Margalit notes that it is possible to live in a civilized society that is not decent. Thus it is important to focus first on decency because it is the conduit through which equity and justice can flow: "A civilized society is one whose members do not humiliate one another" (1996, p. 1).

3 However, in the case of Switzerland it is easier to argue that we are in the presence of a multilingual federation.

4 Rawls, 1972, p. 457.

5 For a similar argument, see Webber, 1994, p. 252.

6 Webber, 1994, pp. 254–255.

7 In the case of Spain, see the works by F. Requejo.

8 Miller, 2000, p. 130; he makes a similar argument in Miller, 2001, pp. 299–318.
9 Miller, 2000, p. 132.
10 See Elazar, 1987, p. 12. See also Burgess, 1993, p. 5.
11 Elazar, 1987, pp. 34–36.
12 See Gagnon, 1993, pp. 15–44.
13 Agranoff, 1999, p. 15.
14 Taylor, 1993a, p. 94.
15 Kymlicka, 1995a, p. 31.
16 Kymlicka, 2001, pp. 114–115.
17 Kymlicka, 1998a, p. 135
18 With respect to healthcare, see Gagnon and Segal, eds, 1999.
19 Ryan, 1999, p. 222.
20 Watts, 2000, p. 49.
21 Smith, 2002, pp. 40–58.
22 Noël, 2006, pp. 305–338.
23 Laforest, 2002.
24 Castells' work on identities' strength of resistance should be noted. See, among others, his groundbreaking work, *Le pouvoir de l'identité*, 1999.
25 Tully, 2000, pp. 4–5.
26 This point is made convincingly by Tully in "Liberté et dévoilement dans les sociétés multinationales", 1999, p. 30.
27 Tully, 2001, p. 33.
28 Bauböck, 2000, p. 383.
29 Bauböck, 2000, p. 383.
30 Kymlicka, 1995a, pp. 76, 80.
31 I have made a similar argument in Gagnon, 2001, pp. 14–27.
32 Held, 2000 p. 23.
33 See the work of H. Meadwell, including Meadwell, 2003, pp. 219–238.
34 See Kymlicka, 1998a, p. 135.
35 For theoretical advances supporting this position, see the GRSP's work.
36 Whitaker, 1992, p. 193.
37 Taylor, 1993a, p. 94.
38 Ignatieff, 2001, p. 84.
39 I doubt the central government's Clarity Bill contributes in any way to encouraging a feeling of trust between Québec and Canada, to the contrary. See F. Rocher and N. Verrelli as well as S. Tierney in *Conditions of Diversity in Multinational Democracies*, 2003.

Conclusion

1 Dumont, 1995, p. 252.
2 As we have seen throughout this book, the work of M. Burgess (the United Kingdom), F. Requejo (Spain) and J. Tully (Canada) on comparative federalism certainly best reflects our assessment of contemporary federalism and modern constitutionalism. See, among others, Burgess, 2006; Requejo, 2003; and Tully, 1995b.
3 Hall, 1996, p. 444.
4 Major work has been done in this sense by some Québécois and Catalan

authors. See Fossas and Requejo, eds, 1999; Gagnon and Iacovino, 2007; and Gagnon *et al.*, 2003.

5 Cohen, 1995, p. 233; see also Dieckhoff, 2004.
6 Todorov, 2006, pp. 114–115 [our translation].
7 Todorov, 2006, pp. 114–115 [our translation].
8 For an analysis that is relatively close to this interpretation, see Ferry, 1998, pp. 169–217.
9 See the work by A.-G. Gagnon and L. Turgeon, among others, in "La bureaucratie représentative au sein des États multinationaux", fall 2006.
10 Todorov, 2006, p. 123 [our translation].
11 R. Maiz's work is very enlightening on this topic. See, among others, Maiz, 2005, pp. 18–23.

Bibliography

Adam, Marc-Antoine, "The Creation of the Council of the Federation", Working Paper, Kingston: Institute of Intergovernmental Relations, Queen's University, Democracy Series, 1, 2005.

Agranoff, Robert, "Power Shifts, Diversity and Asymmetry", in Robert Agranoff, ed., *Accommodating Diversity: Asymmetry in Federal States*, Baden-Baden: Nomos Verlagsgesellschaft, 1999, pp. 120–136.

Ajzenstat, Janet, "Decline of Procedural Liberalism: the Slippery Slope to Secession", in Joseph H. Carens, ed., *Is Quebec Nationalism Just? Perspective from Anglophone Canada*, Montréal and Kingston: McGill-Queen's University Press, 1995, pp. 120–136.

Anderson, Benedict, *L'imaginaire national. Réflexions sur l'origine et l'essor du nationalisme*, Paris: La Découverte, 1996.

Arès, Richard, *La confédération: pacte ou loi?*, new edition, Montréal: Bellarmin, 1967.

Aubarell, Gemma, Nicolau Coll, Agusti and Ross, Adela, eds, *Immigracio i qüestio nacional. Minories subestatals i immigracio a Europa*, Barcelona: Editorial Mediterrania, 2004.

Bakvis, Herman and Skogstad, Grace, eds, *Canadian Federalism: Performance, Effectiveness, and Legitimacy*, 1st edition, Toronto: Oxford University Press, 2002.

Balcells, Albert, *El nacionalismo catalan*, Madrid: Historia 16, 1991.

Balcells, Albert, Pujol Gonzalez, Enric and Sabater, Josdi, *La mancommunitat de Catalunya i l'autonomia*, Barcelona: Proa, 1996.

Balthazar, Louis, "Les relations internationales du Québec", in Alain-G. Gagnon, ed., *Québec: État et Société*, vol. 2, Montréal: Québec Amérique, "Débats" collection, 2003, pp. 505–536.

Bariteau, Claude, "L'Acte de Québec (1774), assise de l'*Indirect rule* toujours d'actualité", in *L'Action nationale*, April 2000, pp. 65–75.

Bariteau, Claude *et al.*, *Les objections de 20 spécialistes aux offres fédérales*, Montréal: Éditions Saint-Martin, 1992.

Bashevkin, Sylvia, *True Patriot Love: the Politics of Canadian Nationalism*, Toronto: Oxford University Press, 1991.

Bastien, Frédéric, *Relations particulières*, Montréal: Boréal, 1999.

Bauböck, Rainer, "Why Stay Together? A Pluralist Approach to Secession and Federation", in Will Kymlicka and Wayne Norman, eds, *Citizenship in Divided Societies*, Oxford: Oxford University Press, 2000, pp. 366–394.

Beauchemin, Jacques, *La société des identités: éthique et politique dans le monde contemporain*, Montréal: Éditions Athéna, 2004.

Belliveau, Joel, "Les bases plurielles des nationalismes périphériques: le cas de la Catalogne", *Canadian Review of Studies in Nationalism*, 29, 1–2, 2002, pp. 27–37.

Bickerton, James, Brooks, Stephen and Gagnon, Alain-G., *Six penseurs en quête de liberté, d'égalité et de communauté*, Québec: Les Presses de l'Université Laval, 2003.

Bickerton, James, Brooks, Stephen and Gagnon, Alain-G., *Freedom, Equality, Community: the Political Philosophy of Six Influential Canadians*, Montréal and Kingston: McGill-Queen's University Press, 2006.

Bickerton, James, Gagnon, Alain-G. and Smith, Patrick, *Partis politiques et comportement électoral au Canada. Filiations et affiliations*, Montréal: Boréal, 2002.

Bouchard, Gérard, *Genèse des nations et cultures du nouveau monde. Essai d'histoire comparée*, Montréal: Boréal, 2000.

Brock, Kathy, "The Politics of Process", in Douglas Brown, ed., *Canada: the State of the Federation, 1991*, Kingston: Institute of Intergovernmental Relations, 1991, pp. 57–87.

Brock, Kathy, "The End of Executive Federalism", in François Rocher and Miriam Smith, eds, *New Trends in Canadian Federalism*, 1st edition, Peterborough: Broadview Press, 1995, pp. 91–108.

Brock, Kathy, "Executive Federalism: Beggar Thy Neighbour?", in François Rocher and Miriam Smith, eds, *New Trends in Canadian Federalism*, 2nd edition, Peterborough: Broadview Press, 2003, pp. 67–83.

Brubaker, Rogers, *Nationalism Reframed: Nationhood and the National Question in the New Europe*, Cambridge: Cambridge University Press, 1996.

Burelle, André, *Le mal canadien: essai de diagnostic et esquisse d'une thérapie*, Montréal: Fides, 1995.

Burelle, André, *Le droit à la différence à l'heure de la globalisation: le cas du Québec et du Canada*, Montréal: Fides, 1996.

Burelle, André, "Mise en tutelle des provinces", *Le Devoir*, Montréal, 15 February 1999, p. A-7.

Burelle, André, "The Council of the Federation: From a Defensive to a Partnership Approach", Kingston: Institute of Intergovernmental Relations, 2003.

Burelle, André, *Pierre Elliott Trudeau: L'intellectuel et le politique*, Montréal: Fides, 2005.

Burgess, Michael, *Comparative Federalism: Theory and Practice*, London: Routledge, 2006.

Burgess, Michael and Gagnon, Alain-G., eds, *Federal Democracies*, London: Routledge, forthcoming.

Cairns, Alan C., "Citizens (Outsiders) and Governments (Insiders) in Constitution-Making: the Case of Meech Lake", *Canadian Public Policy*, vol. 14, Supplement 1, 1988, pp. 121–145.

Cairns, Alan C., "Constitutional Change and the Three Equalities", in Ronald Watts and Douglas M. Brown, eds, *Options for a New Canada*, Toronto: University of Toronto Press, 1991, pp. 77–100.

Cairns, Alan C., *Citizens Plus: Aboriginal Peoples and the Canadian State*, Vancouver: University of British Columbia Press, 2000.

Calhoun, Craig, *Nationalism*, Minneapolis: University of Minnesota Press, 1997.

Campuzano Carvajal, Francisco, "L'article 2 de la Constitution de 1978. Une tentative de redéfinition de la nation espagnole ", in Francisco Campuzano Carvajal, ed., *Les nationalisme en Espagne. De l'État libéral à l'État des autonomies (1876–1978)*, Montpellier: Publications Montpellier 3, 2001.

Campuzano Carvajal, Francisco, ed., *Les nationalismes en Espagne. De l'État libéral à l'État des autonomies (1876–1978)*, Montpellier: Publications Montpellier 3, 2001.

Caron, Jean-François, Laforest, Guy and Vallières-Roland, Catherine, "Le déficit fédératif au Canada", in Alain-G. Gagnon, ed., *Le fédéralisme canadien contemporain*, Montréal: Les Presses de l'Université de Montréal, 2006, pp. 147–182.

Cascajo Castro, José Luis, "Notas sobre el ordenamiento constitucional de la Segunda Republica: la distribucion de competencias en el estado integral", *Revista Vasca de Administracion Publica*, 36, 1993, pp. 17–20.

Castells, Manuel, *Le pouvoir de l'identité*, Paris: Fayard, 1999.

Castineira, Angel, "Identitat, reconeixement. Un debat al voltant de Charles Taylor", in Ferran Requejo, ed., *Pluralisme nacional i legitimitat democratica*, Barcelona: Proa, 1999, pp. 111–114.

Chevrier, Marc, "La genèse de l'idée fédérale chez les pères fondateurs américains et canadiens", in Alain-G. Gagnon, ed., *Le fédéralisme canadien contemporain*, Montréal: Les Presses de l'Université de Montréal, 2006, pp. 19–61.

Citizen's Forum on Canada's Future, *Citizen's Forum on Canada's Future: Report to the People and Government of Canada*, Ottawa: Canadian Government Publishing Centre, 1991.

Cohen, Mitchell, "Rooted Cosmopolitanism", in Michael Walzer, ed., *Toward a Global Civil Society*, Oxford: Berghahn, 1995, pp. 223–233.

Commission des États généraux sur la situation et l'avenir de la langue française au Québec (Larose Commission), *Le français, une langue pour tout le monde, une nouvelle approche stratégique et citoyenne*, Québec City: Government of Québec, 2001.

de Villiers, Bertus, ed., *Evaluating Federal Systems*, Cape Town/Dordrecht: Juta & Co./Martinus Nijhoff Publishers, 1994.

de Villiers, Bertus, *Bundestreue: the Soul of an Intergovernmental Partnership*, Johannesburg: Konrad Adenauer Stiftung, Occasional papers, 1995.

Delgamuukw v. *British Columbia* (1997) 3 S.C.R. 1010.

Delpérée, Francis, "Le fédéralisme sauvera-t-il la nation belge?", in Jacques Rupnick, ed., *Le déchirement des nations*, Paris: Éditions du Seuil, 1995, pp. 123–137.

Dieckhoff, Alain, ed. *La constellation des appartenances. Nationalisme, libéralisme et pluralisme*, Paris: Les Presses de Sciences Po, 2004.

Dumont, Fernand, *Genèse de la société québécoise*, Montréal: Boréal, 1993.

Dumont, Fernand, *Raisons communes*, Montréal: Boréal, 1995.

Eisenberg, Avigail, "The Politics of Individual and Group Difference in Canadian Jurisprudence", *Canadian Journal of Political Science*, 27, 1, 1994, pp. 3–21.

Elazar, Daniel, *Exploring Federalism*, Tuscaloosa: University of Alabama Press, 1987.

Facal, Joseph, "Mondialisation, identités et fédéralisme. A propos de la mutation du système politique canadien", in Alain-G. Gagnon, ed., *Le fédéralisme canadien contemporain*, Montréal: Les Presses de l'Université de Montréal, 2006, pp. 237–249.

Ferry, Jean-Marc, "L'État européen", in Riva Kastoryano, ed., *Quelle identité pour l'Europe? Le multiculturalisme à l'épreuve*, Paris: Les Presses de Sciences Po, 1998, pp. 169–217.

Flanagan, Tom, *First Nations? Second Thoughts*, Montréal and Kingston: McGill-Queen's University Press, 2000.

Fortin, Sarah, "De l'union sociale canadienne à l'union sociale fédérale du Canada", in Alain-G. Gagnon, ed., *Le fédéralisme canadien contemporain. Fondements, traditions, institutions*, Montréal: Les Presses de l'Université de Montréal, 2006, pp. 339–369.

Fossas, Enric, "Asimetria y plurinacionalidad en el estado autonomico", in Enric Fossas and Ferran Requejo, eds, *Asimetria federal y estado plurinacional*, Barcelona: Editorial Trotta, 1999.

Fossas, Enric and Requejo, Ferran, eds, *Asimetria Federal Y Estado Plurinacional. El Debate Sobre la Acomodacion de la Diversidad en Canada, Belgica Y Espana*, Madrid: Editorial Trotta, 1999.

Gagné, Gilles and Langlois, Simon, "Les jeunes appuient la souveraineté et les souverainistes le demeurent en vieillissant", *L'annuaire du Québec 2006*, Montréal: Fides, 2006, pp. 440–456.

Gagnon, Alain-G., "The Political Uses of Federalism", in Michael Burgess and Alain-G. Gagnon, eds, *Comparative Federalism and Federation: Competing Traditions and Future Directions*, Toronto and London: University of Toronto Press and Harvester and Wheatsheaf, 1993, pp. 15–44.

Gagnon, Alain-G., "Québec–Canada; circonvolutions constitutionnelles", in Alain-G. Gagnon, ed., *Québec: État et société*, vol. 1, Montréal: Québec Amérique, 1994, pp. 85–106.

Gagnon, Alain-G., *Quebec y el federalismo canadiense*, Madrid: Consejo superior de investigaciones cientificas, 1998.

Gagnon, Alain-G., "Le Québec, entre l'État-nation et l'État-région", *Le Devoir*, 25 July 2000a, p. A-7.

Gagnon, Alain-G., "Travailler en partenariat pour les Canadiens", in Alain-G. Gagnon, ed., *L'Union sociale sans le Québec. Huit études sur l'entente-cadre*, Montréal: Les Éditions Saint-Martin, 2000b, pp. 129–154.

Gagnon, Alain-G., "Quebec: the Emergence of a Region-State?", *Scottish Affairs*, Special Issue, "Stateless Nations in the 21st Century: Scotland, Catalonia and Quebec", 2001, pp. 14–27.

Gagnon, Alain-G., "Le dossier constitutionnel Québec-Canada", *Québec: État et société*, vol. 2, Montréal: Québec Amérique, "Débats" collection, 2003a, pp. 151–174.

Gagnon, Alain-G., "Undermining Federalism and Feeding Minority National-ism: the Impact of Majority Nationalism in Canada", in Alain-G. Gagnon, Montserrat Guibernau and François Rocher, eds, *The Conditions of Diver-sity in Multinational Democracies*, Montréal: Institute for Research on Public Policy/McGill-Queen's University Press, 2003b, pp. 295–312.

Gagnon, Alain-G., "Le fédéralisme asymétrique au Canada", in Alain-G. Gagnon, ed., *Le fédéralisme canadien contemporain*, Montréal: Les Presses de l'Université de Montréal, 2006, pp. 287–304.

Gagnon, Alain-G. and Chokri, Laurent-Mehdi, "Le régime politique canad-ien: histoire et enjeux", in Réjean Pelletier and Manon Tremblay, eds, *Le parlementarisme canadien*, 3rd edition, Québec: Les Presses de l'Université Laval, 2005, pp. 9–35.

Gagnon, Alain-G. and Garcea, Joseph, "Quebec and the Pursuit of Special Status", in R. D. Olling and M.W. Westmacott, eds, *Perspectives on Cana-dian Federalism*, Scarborough: Prentice-Hall Canada, 1988, pp. 304–325.

Gagnon, Alain-G. and Iacovino, Raffaele, *Federalism, Citizenship, and Quebec: Debating Multinationalism*, Toronto: University of Toronto Press, 2007.

Gagnon, Alain-G. and Laforest, Guy, "The Future of Federalism: Lessons from Quebec and Canada", *International Journal*, 48, 3, 1993, pp. 468–491.

Gagnon, Alain-G. and Latouche, Daniel, *Allaire, Bélanger, Campeau et les autres. Les Québécois s'interrogent sur leur avenir*, Montréal: Québec Amérique, 1991.

Gagnon, Alain-G. and Montcalm, Mary Beth, *Au-delà de la révolution tran-quille*, Montréal: VLB éditeur, 1992.

Gagnon, Alain-G. and Segal, Hugh, eds, *The Canadian Social Union Without Quebec: 8 Critical Analyses*, Montreal: Institute for Research on Public Policy, 1999.

Gagnon, Alain-G. and Tully, James, eds, *Multinational Democracies*, Cam-bridge: Cambridge University Press, 2001.

Gagnon, Alain-G. and Turgeon, Luc, "Managing Diversity in Eighteenth- and Nineteenth-Century Canada: Québec's Constitutional Development in Light of the Scottish Experience", *The Journal of Commonwealth and Comparative Politics*, 41, 1, 2003, pp. 1–23.

144　*Bibliography*

Gagnon, Alain-G. and Turgeon, Luc, "La bureaucratie représentative au sein des États multinationaux", *Revue française d'administration publique*, 118, fall 2006, pp. 291–306.

Gagnon, Alain-G., Guibernau, Montserrat and Rocher, François, eds, *The Conditions of Diversity in Multinational Democracies*, Montréal: Institute of Research on Public Policy, 2003.

Gaudreault-Desbiens, Jean-François, *Les compartiments étanches du bijuridisme au Canada. Essai sur la résilience des atavismes juridiques*, Montréal: Themis, 2006.

Giner, Salvador, ed., *La societat catalana*, Barcelona: Institut d'Estadistica de Catalunya, 1998.

Gouvernement du Québec, *Commission sur l'avenir politique et constitutionnel du Québec*, Québec: Publications officielles du Québec, 1991.

Government of Québec, Conseil des communautés culturelles et de l'immigration, "Culture publique commune et cohésion sociale: le 'contrat moral' d'intégration des immigrants dans un Québec francophone, démocratique et pluraliste", in *Gérer la diversité dans un Québec francophone, démocratique et pluraliste. Principes de fond et de procédure pour guider la recherche d'accommodements raisonnables*, 1993.

Greenfeld, Liah, *Nationalism: Five Roads to Modernity*, Cambridge: Harvard University Press, 1992.

Greenfeld, Liah, *Nationalism and the Mind: Essays on Modern Culture*, Oxford: Oneworld Publications, 2006.

Guerena, Jean-Louis, "État et nation en Espagne au XIXe siècle", in Francisco Campuzano Carvajal, ed., *De l'État libéral à l'État des autonomies (1876–1978)*, Montpellier: Publications Montpellier 3, 2001, pp. 17–38.

Guibernau, Montserrat, *Catalan Nationalism: Francoism, Transition and Democracy*, Cambridge: Polity Press, 2002.

Gutmann, Amy, *Identity and Democracy*, Princeton: Princeton University Press, 2003.

Hall, Stuart, "New Ethnicities", in David Morley and Kuan-Hsing Chen, eds, *Stuart Hall: Critical Dialogues in Cultural Studies*, London: Routledge, 1996, pp. 441–449.

Harty, Siobhan and Murphy, Michael, *In Defence of Multinational Citizenship*, Vancouver: University of British Columbia Press, 2005.

Held, David, "The Changing Contours of Political Community: Rethinking Democracy in the Context of Globalization", in Barry Holden, ed., *Global Democracy: Key Debates*, London: Routledge, 2000, pp. 17–31.

Herrero de Minon, Miguel, "La posible diversidad de los modelos autonomicos en la transicion", Institut d'Estudis Autonomics, *Uniformidad o diversidad de las Communidades Autonomas*, Barcelona, 1995.

Hiebert, Janet L., *Limiting Rights: the Dilemma of Judicial Review*, Montréal and Kingston: McGill-Queen's University Press, 1996.

Ignatieff, Michael, *The Rights Revolution*, Toronto: House of Anansi Press Ltd, 2001.

Jacob, Steve, "Le fédéralisme conflictuel: identité régionale et gestion des conflits en Belgique", in Hélène Pauliat, ed., *L'autonomie des collectivités territoriales en Europe: une source potentielle de conflits?*, Limoges: Les Presses de l'Université de Limoges, 2004, pp. 239–266.

Jedwab, Jack, "Notional Nations: the Myth of Canada as a Multinational Federation", in *Canadian Diversity*, 3, 2, Spring 2004, p. 20.

Jenson, Jane, "Naming Nations: Making Nationalist Claims in Canadian Public Discourse", *Canadian Journal of Sociology and Anthropology*, 30, 3, 1993, pp. 337–358.

Jenson, Jane, "Recognizing Difference: Distinct Societies, Citizenship Regimes and Partnership", in Guy Laforest and Roger Gibbins, eds, *Beyond the Impasse: Toward Reconciliation*, Montréal: Institute for Research on Public Policy, 1998, pp. 215–239.

Jouve, Bernard and Gagnon, Alain-G., eds, *Les métropoles au défi de la diversité culturelle*, Grenoble: Les Presses universitaires de Grenoble, 2006.

Karmis, Dimitrios, "Pluralisme et identité(s) nationale(s) dans le Québec contemporain", in Alain-G. Gagnon, ed., *Québec: État et société*, vol. 2, Montréal, Québec Amérique, "Débats" collection, 2003, pp. 85–116.

Karmis, Dimitrios, "Les multiples voix de la tradition fédérale et la tourmente du fédéralisme canadien", in Alain-G. Gagnon, ed., *Le fédéralisme canadien contemporain*, Montréal: Les Presses de l'Université de Montréal, 2006, pp. 63–91.

Karmis, Dimitrios and Norman, Wayne, "The Revival of Federalism in Normative Political Theory", in Dimitrios Karmis and Wayne Norman, eds, *Theories of Federalism*, New York: Palgrave Macmillan, 2005, pp. 63–91.

Keating, Michael, *Les défis du nationalisme moderne. Québec, Catalogne, Écosse*, Montréal: Les Presses de l'Université de Montréal, 1997.

Keating, Michael, *Nations Against the State: the New Politics of Nation in Québec, Catalonia and Scotland*, 2nd edition, Houndmills, Basingstoke: Palgrave, 2001a.

Keating, Michael, *Plurinational Democracy: Stateless Nations in a Post-Sovereignty Era*, Oxford: Oxford University Press, 2001b.

Keohane, Robert O., *After Hegemony: Cooperation and Discord in the World Political Economy*, Princeton: Princeton University Press, 1984.

Kernerman, Gerald, *Multicultural Nationalism: Civilizing Difference, Constituting Community*, Vancouver: University of British Columbia Press, 2005.

Ketcham, Ralph, ed., *The Anti-Federalist Papers and the Constitutional Convention Debates*, New York: Penguin, 1986.

King, Preston, *Federalism and Federation*, Baltimore: Johns Hopkins University Press, 1982.

Knopff, Rainer and Morton, Fred L., "Nation-Building and the Canadian Charter of Rights and Freedoms", in Alan Cairns and Cynthia Williams, eds, *Constitutionalism, Citizenship and Society in Canada*, Toronto: University of Toronto Press, 1985, pp. 133–182.

Kukathas, Chandran, "Are There Any Cultural Rights?", *Political Theory*, 20, 1992, pp. 105–139.

Kymlicka, Will, *Multicultural Citizenship*, New York: Oxford University Press, 1995a.

Kymlicka, Will, "The Paradox of Liberal Nationalism", *Literary Review of Canada*, November 1995b, p. 15.

Kymlicka, Will, ed., *The Rights of Minority Cultures*, New York: Oxford University Press, 1995c.

Kymlicka, Will, *Finding Our Way: Rethinking Ethnocultural Relations in Canada*, Toronto: Oxford University Press, 1998a.

Kymlicka, Will, "Is Federalism a Viable Alternative to Secession?", in Percy B. Lehning, ed., *Theories of Secession*, London: Routledge, 1998b, pp. 111–150.

Kymlicka, Will, "Multinational Federalism in Canada: Rethinking the Partnership", *Policy Options*, March 1998c, pp. 5–9.

Kymlicka, Will, *Politics in the Vernacular: Nationalism, Multiculturalism, and Citizenship*, Oxford: Oxford University Press, 2001.

Kymlicka, Will and Raviot, Jean-Robert, "Vie commune, aspects internationaux des fédéralismes", *Études internationales*, 28, 4, 1997, pp. 779–843.

Lacasta-Zabalda, José Ignacio, *Espana uniforme*, Gobierno de Navarra: Departemento de educacion y cultura, 1998.

Laforest, Guy, *Trudeau et la fin d'un rêve canadien*, Québec: Les Éditions du Septentrion, 1992.

Laforest, Guy, "Se placer dans les souiliers des autres partenaires dans l'union canadienne", in Guy Laforest and Roger Gibbins, eds, *Sortir de l'impasse*, Montréal: Institut de recherche en politiques publiques, 1998, pp. 55–84.

Laforest, Guy, "Le ministre Dion, la Charte des droits et l'avenir du Québec", *Le Soleil*, 26 April 2002.

Lahaise, Robert and Vallerand, Noël, *Le Québec sous le régime anglais*, Montréal: Lanctôt éditeur, 1999.

Lajoie, Andrée, "Le fédéralisme au Canada," in Alain-G. Gagnon, ed., *Le fédéralisme canadien contemporain*, Montréal: Les Presses de l'Université de Montréal, 2006, pp. 183–209.

Langlois, Simon, "Le choc de deux sociétés globales", in Louis Balthazar, Guy Laforest and Vincent Lemieux, eds, *Le Québec et la restructuration du Canada, 1980–1992*, Québec City: Septentrion, 1991, pp. 95–108.

LaSelva, Samuel, *The Moral Foundations of Canadian Federalism: Paradoxes, Achievements, and Tragedies of Nationhood*, Montréal and Kingston: McGill-Queen's University Press, 1996.

Latouche, Daniel, "State Building and Foreign Policy at the Subnational Level", in Ivo D. Duchacek, Daniel Latouche and Garth Stevenson, eds, *Perforated Sovereignties and International Relations: Trans-Sovereign Contacts of Subnational Governments*, Westport: Greenwood Press, 1988, pp. 29–42.

Lazar, Harvey, "Non-Constitutional Renewal: Towards a New Equilibrium in the Federation", in Harvey Lazar, ed., *The State of the Federation, 1997*, Kingston: Institute of Intergovernmental Relations, 1998, pp. 3–35.

Lazar, Harvey, "Managing Interdependencies in the Canadian Federation:

Lessons from the Social Union Framework Agreement", Working Paper, Institute of Intergovernmental Relations, Queen's University, 2003.

Lenihan, Donald, Robertson, Gordon and Tassé, Roger, *Canada: Reclaiming the Middle Ground*, Montréal: Institute for Research on Public Policy, 1994.

Leroy, Michel, *De la Belgique unitaire à l'État fédéral*, Bruxelles: Bruylant, 1996.

Leton, André and Miroir, André, *Les conflits communautaires en Belgique*, Paris: Les Presses Universitaires de France, 1999.

Lijphart, Arend, *The Politics of Accommodation: Pluralism and Democracy in the Netherlands*, Berkeley: University of California Press, 1968.

Lijphart, Arend, *Democracy in Plural Societies: a Comparative Exploration.* New Haven: Yale University Press, 1977.

Lijphart, Arend, "Consociation: the Model and its Application in Divided Societies", in Desmond Rae, ed., *Political Co-operation in Divided Societies*, Dublin: Gill and Macmillan, 1982, pp. 166–186.

Linz, Juan, *Democracy, Multinationalism and Federalism (Working Paper No. 103)*, Madrid: Centro de Estudios Avanzados en Ciencias Sociales, Instituto Juan March, 1997.

Livingston, William S., "A Note on the Nature of Federalism", *Political Science Quarterly*, 67, March 1952, pp. 81–95.

Loughlin, John, *Subnational Democracy in the European Union*, Oxford: Oxford University Press, 2001.

Loughlin, John, "Les nationalismes britannique et français face aux défis de l'européanisation et la mondialisation", in Alain-G. Gagnon, André Lecours and Geneviève Nootens, eds, *Les nationalismes majoritaires contemporains*, Montréal: Québec Amérique, 2007, pp. 197–215.

MacInnes, John and McCrone, David, eds, *Scottish Affairs*, "Stateless Nations in the 21st Century: Scotland, Catalonia and Quebec", Special issue, no. 37, Autumn 2001.

Maclure, Jocelyn and Gagnon, Alain-G., eds, *Repères en mutation: identité et citoyenneté dans le Québec contemporain*, Montréal: Québec Amérique, "Débats" collection, 2001.

Maclure, Jocelyn and Karmis, Dimitrios, "Two Escape Routes from the Paradigm of Monistic Authenticity: Post-Imperial and Federal Perspectives on Plural Identities", *Ethnic and Racial Studies*, 24, 3, 2001, pp. 361–385.

McRae, Kenneth, "Le concept de la société fragmentaire de Louis Hartz: son application à l'exemple canadien", *Revue canadienne de théorie politique et sociale*, 3, 3, 1979a, pp. 69–82.

McRae, Kenneth, "The Plural Society and the Western Political Tradition", *Canadian Journal of Political Science*, 12, 4, 1979b, pp. 675–688.

McRae, Kenneth, *Conflict and Compromise in Multilingual Societies: Switzerland*, Waterloo: Wilfrid Laurier University Press, 1983.

McRae, Kenneth, *Conflict and Compromise in Multilingual Societies: Belgium*, Waterloo: Wilfrid Laurier University Press, 1986.

McRoberts, Kenneth, *Misconceiving Canada*, Don Mills: Oxford University Press, 1997.

McRoberts, Kenneth, *Un pays à refaire: l'échec des politiques constitution-nelles canadiennes*, Montréal: Les Éditions du Boréal, 1999.

Maiz, Ramon, "Nacion de naciones y federalismo", *Claves de Razon Practica*, 157, November 2005, pp. 18–23.

Maiz, Ramon and Requejo, Ferran, eds, *Democracy, Nationalism and Multiculturalism*, London: Routledge, 2005.

Margalit, Avishai, *The Decent Society*, Cambridge: Harvard University Press, 1996.

Meadwell, Hudson, "Is a 'True' Multinational Federation a Cure for Our Ills?", in Patrick James, Donald E. Abelson and Michael Lusztig, eds, *The Myth of the Sacred: the Charter, the Courts, and the Politics of the Constitution in Canada*, Montréal and Kingston: McGill-Queen's University Press, 2003, pp. 219–238.

Meisel, John and Rocher, Guy, eds, *As I recalled. Si je me souviens bien. Regards sur l'histoire*, Montréal: Institute for Research on Public Policy, 1999.

Miller, David, *On Nationality*, Oxford: Oxford University Press, 1995.

Miller, David, *Citizenship and National Identity*, Cambridge: Polity Press, 2000.

Miller, David, "Nationality in Divided Societies", in Alain-G. Gagnon and James Tully, eds, *Multinational Democracies*, Cambridge: Cambridge University Press, 2001, pp. 299–318.

Milne, David E., "Equality or Asymmetry: Why Choose?", in Ronald L. Watts and Douglas M. Brown, eds, *Options for a New Canada*, Toronto: University of Toronto Press, 1991, pp. 285–307.

Molas, Isidre, *Ideario de Francisco Pi Y Margall*, Madrid: Ediciones Peninsula, 1966.

Montesquieu, *The Spirit of Laws*, Part I, Book VIII, trans. Thomas Nugent (J.V. Pritchard), 1849.

Moreno, Luis, *The Federalization of Spain*, London: Frank Cass Publishers, 2001.

Moreno, Luis, Arriba, Ana and Serrano, Araceli, *Multiple Identities in Decentralized Spain: The Case of Catalonia*, Madrid: Instituto de Estudios Sociales Avanzados (CSIS), Working Paper 97-06, 1998.

Neatby, Hilda, *The Québec Act: Protest and Policy*, Scarborough: Prentice-Hall of Canada, 1972.

Noël, Alain, "Le principe fédéral, la solidarité et le partenariat", in Guy Laforest and Roger Gibbins, eds, *Sortir de l'impasse: les voies de la réconciliation*, Montréal: Institute for Research on Public Policy, 1998, pp. 263–295.

Noël, Alain, "Without Quebec: Collaborative Federalism with a Footnote", *Policy Matters*, 1, 2, March 2000, pp. 1–26.

Noël, Alain, "Democratic Deliberation in Multinational Federation", Paper presented at the 2003 Annual Meetings of the Canadian Political Science Association, Dalhousie University, Halifax, May–June 2003.

Noël, Alain, "Équilibres et déséquilibres dans le partage des ressources financières", in Alain-G. Gagnon, ed., *Le fédéralisme canadien contemporain*, Montréal: Les Presses de l'Université de Montréal, 2006, pp. 305–338.

Nootens, Geneviève, *Désenclaver la démocratie. Des huguenots à la Paix des Braves*, Montréal: Québec Amérique, "Débats" collection, 2004.

Nunez Seixas, Xosé Manoel, *Los nacionalismos en la Espana contemporanea Siglos XIX–XX*, Barcelona: Hipotesi, 1999.

Oliver, Michael, "Laurendeau et Trudeau: leurs opinions sur le Canada", in Raymond Hudon and Réjean Pelletier, eds, *L'engagement intellectuel: mélanges en l'honneur de Léon Dion*, Sainte-Foy: Les Presses de l'Université Laval, 1991, pp. 339–368.

Pal, Leslie, *Interests of State: the Politics of Language, Multiculturalism and Feminism in Canada*, Montréal and Kingston: McGill-Queen's University Press, 1993.

Pal, Leslie A. and Seidle, Leslie, "Constitutional Politics 1990–92: the Paradox of Participation", in Susan D. Phillips, ed., *How Ottawa Spends: a More Democratic Government...?* Ottawa: Carleton University Press, 1993, pp. 143–202.

Papillon, Martin, "Vers un fédéralisme postcolonial? La difficile rédéfinition des rapports entre l'État canadien et les peuples autochtones", in Alain-G. Gagnon, ed., *Le fédéralisme canadien contemporain*, Montréal: Les Presses de l'Université de Montréal, 2006, pp. 113–140.

Papillon, Martin and Simeon, Richard, "The Weakest Link? First Ministers' Conferences in Canadian Intergovernmental Relations", in J. Peter Meekison, Hamish Telford and Harvey Lazar, eds, *Canada: the State of the Federation 2002. Reconsidering the Institutions of Canadian Federalism*, Kingston: Queen's Institute of Intergovernmental Relations, 2004, pp. 461–485.

Paquin, Stéphane, *Paradiplomatie et relations internationales: Théorie des stratégies internationales des régions face à la mondialisation*, Brussels: Les Presses interuniversitaires européennes/Peter Lang, 2004.

Paquin, Stéphane, ed., *Le prolongement externe des compétences internes: les relations internationales du Québec depuis la doctrine Gérin-Lajoie (1965–2005)*, Québec City: Les Presses de l'Université Laval, 2006.

Pierré-Caps, Stéphane, *La multination. L'avenir des minorités en Europe centrale et orientale*, Paris: Éditions Odile Jacob, 1995.

Porter, John, *The Vertical Mosaic: an Analysis of Social Class and Power in Canada*, Toronto: University of Toronto Press, 1965.

Presthus, Robert, *Elite Accommodation in Canadian Politics*, Toronto: Macmillan Canada, 1973.

Proudhon, Pierre Joseph, *The Principle of Federation*, trans. Richard Vernon, Toronto: University of Toronto Press, 1979.

Rabushka, Alvin and Shepsle, Kenneth A., "Political Entrepreneurship and Patterns of Democratic Instability in Plural Societies", *Race*, 12, 4, 1971, pp. 461–476.

Rawls, John, *A Theory of Justice*, Oxford: Oxford University Press, 1972.

Rawls, John, *Political Liberalism*, New York: Columbia University Press, 1993.

Requejo, Ferran, *Federalisme, per a què? L'acomodacio de la diversitat en democracies plurinationals*, Barcelona: L'Hora del present, 1998.

Requejo, Ferran, "Cultural Pluralism, Nationalism and Federalism: a Revision of Democratic Citizenship in Plurinational States", *European Journal of Political Research*, 35, 2, March 1999, pp. 255–286.

Requejo, Ferran, *Federalisme plurinacional i estat de les autonomies: Aspectes teòrics i aplicats*, Barcelona: Proa, 2003.

Requejo, Ferran, *Multinational Federalism and Value Pluralism*, London: Routledge, 2005.

Resnick, Philip, *Thinking English Canada*, Toronto: Stoddard, 1994a.

Resnick, Philip, "Toward a Multinational Federalism: Asymmetrical and Confederal Alternatives", in Leslie Seidle, ed., *À la recherche d'un nouveau contrat politique: options asymétriques et options confédérales*, Montréal: Institute for Research on Public Policy, 1994b, pp. 71–90.

Rioux, Christian, *Voyage à l'intérieur des petites nations*, Montréal: Boréal, 2000.

Rupnik, Jacques, ed., *Le déchirement des nations*, Paris: Seuil, 1995.

Russell, Peter H., "Conclusion", *Nationalism in Canada*, in Peter H. Russell, ed., Toronto: McGraw-Hill, 1966.

Russell, Peter H., "Bold Statecraft, Questionable Jurisprudence", in Keith Banting and Richard Simeon, eds, *And No One Cheered*, Toronto: Methuen, 1983a, pp. 210–238.

Russell, Peter H., "The Political Purposes of the Charter of Rights and Freedoms", *Canadian Bar Review*, 61, 1983b, pp. 1–33.

Russell, Peter H., *Constitutional Odyssey: Can Canadians Become a Sovereign People?*, 2nd edition, Toronto: University of Toronto Press, 1993.

Russell, Peter H., *Constitutional Odyssey: Can Canadians Become a Sovereign People?*, 3rd edition, Toronto: University of Toronto Press, 2004.

Ryan, C., "The Agreement on the Canadian Social Union as Seen by a Quebec Federalist", in Gagnon, Alain-G. and Segal, Hugh, eds, *The Canadian Social Union Without Quebec: 8 Critical Analyses*, Montreal: Institute for Research on Public Policy, 1999.

Sánchez-Terán, Salvador, *De Franco à la Generalitat*, Barcelona: Planeta, 1988.

Sandel, Michael, *Liberalism and the Limits of Justice*, 2nd edition, New York: Cambridge University Press, 1989.

Seymour, Michel, *La nation en question*, Montréal: L'Hexagone, 1999.

Seymour, Michel, "La proie pour l'ombre. Les illusions d'une réforme de la fédération canadienne", in Alain-G. Gagnon, ed., *Le fédéralisme canadien contemporain*, Montréal: Les Presses de l'Université de Montréal, 2006, pp. 211–235.

Sheppard, Robert and Valpy, Michael, *The National Debt*, Toronto: Fleet Books, 1982.

Simeon, Richard and Cameron, David, "Intergovernmental Relations and Democracy: an Oxymoron if There Ever Was One", in Herman Bakvis and Grace Skogstad, eds, *Canadian Federalism: Performance, Effectiveness, and Legitimacy*, Toronto: Oxford University Press, 2002, pp. 278–295.

Simeon, Richard and Robinson, Ian, *State, Society, and the Development of Canadian Federalism*, Toronto: University of Toronto Press, 1990.

Simeon, Richard and Robinson, Ian, "The Dynamics of Canadian Federalism", in James Bickerton and Alain-G. Gagnon, eds, *Canadian Politics*, 4th edition, Peterborough: Broadview Press, 2004, pp. 101–126.

Smiley, Donald V., "An Outsider's Observations of Federal–Provincial Relations Among Consenting Adults", in Richard Simeon, ed., *Confrontation and Collaboration: Intergovernmental Relations in Canada Today*, Toronto: Institute of Public Administration of Canada, 1979, pp. 105–112.

Smiley, Donald V., *Canada in Question: Federalism in the Eighties*, Toronto: McGraw-Hill Ryerson, 1980.

Smiley, Donald V., *The Federal Condition in Canada*, Toronto: McGraw-Hill, 1987.

Smith, David E., "Party Government, Representation and National Integration in Canada", in Peter Aucoin, ed., *Party Government and Regional Representation in Canada*, Toronto: University of Toronto Press, 1985, pp. 1–68.

Smith, Graham, "Mapping the Federal Condition: Ideology, Political Practice and Social Justice", in Graham Smith, ed., *Federalism: the Multiethnic Challenge*, London: Longman, 1995, pp. 1–28.

Smith, Jennifer, "Informal Constitutional Development: Change by Other Means", in Herman Bakvis and Grace Skogstad, eds, 1st edition, Don Mills, Ontario: Oxford University Press, 2002, pp. 40–58.

Smith, J., "The Constitutional Debate and Beyond", in F. Rocher and M. Smith, eds, *New Trends in Canadian Federalism*, 2nd edition, Peterborough: Broadview Press, 2003, pp. 45–65.

Smith, Jennifer, *Federalism*, Vancouver: University of British Columbia Press, 2004.

Soldatos, Panayotis, "Les relations internationales du Québec: la marque d'un déterminisme économique", in Denis Monière, ed., *L'année politique au Québec, 1987–1988*, Montréal: Québec Amérique, 1988, 109–123.

Sparaole, Enrico and Alesina, Alberto, *The Size of Nations*, Cambridge: Massachusetts Institute of Technology, 2003.

Spinner, Jeffrey, *The Boundaries of Citizenship: Race, Ethnicity, and Nationality in the Liberal State*, Baltimore: Johns Hopkins University Press, 1994.

Stepan, Alfred, "Federalism and Democracy: Beyond the U.S. Model", *Journal of Democracy*, 10, 4, 1999, pp. 19–34.

Swinton, Katherine E. and Rogerson, Carol J., eds, *Competing Constitutional Visions*, Toronto: Carswell, 1988.

Tamir, Yael, *Liberal Nationalism*, Princeton: Princeton University Press, 1993.

Taylor, Charles, "Atomism", *Philosophy and the Human Sciences: Philosophical Papers*, 2, Cambridge: Cambridge University Press, 1985, pp. 187–210.

Taylor, Charles, "The Deep Challenge of Dualism", in Alain-G. Gagnon, ed., *Quebec: State and Society*, 2nd edition, Scarborough: Nelson Canada, 1993a, pp. 82–95.

Taylor, Charles, *Reconciling the Solitudes: Essays on Canadian Federalism and Nationalism*, Montréal and Kingston: McGill-Queen's University Press, 1993b.

Taylor, Charles, *Multiculturalisme. Différence et démocratie*, Paris: Flammarion, 1994a, 42–99.

Taylor, Charles, "The Politics of Recognition", in Amy Gutmann, ed., *Multiculturalism*, Princeton: Princeton University Press, 1994b.

Thérien, Jean-Philippe, Bélanger, Louis and Gosselin, Guy, "La politique étrangère québécoise", in Alain-G. Gagnon, ed., *Québec: État et société*, vol. 1, Montréal: Québec Amérique, 1994, pp. 259–278.

Tierney, Stephen, *Constitutional Law and National Pluralism*, Oxford: Oxford University Press, 2004.

Todorov, Tzvetan, *Devoirs et délices. Une vie de passeur*, Paris: Seuil, 2002.

Todorov, Tzvetan, *L'Esprit des Lumières*, Paris: Robert Laffont, 2006.

Trudeau, Pierre Elliott, *Federalism and the French Canadians*, Toronto: Macmillan, 1968.

Trudeau, Pierre Elliott, *L'épreuve du droit: le débat sur la souveraineté canadienne*, Toronto: Harper Collins Publishers, 1991.

Trujillo, Gurmensindo, *Introduccion al federalismo espanol*, Madrid: Editorial Cuadernos para el Dialogo, 1967.

Tully, James, "The Crisis of Identification: the Case of Canada", *Political Studies*, 42, 1992, pp. 77–96.

Tully, James, "Diversity's Gambit Declined", in Curtis Cook, ed., *Constitutional Predicament: Canada After the Referendum of 1992*, Montréal and Kingston: McGill-Queen's University Press, 1994a, pp. 157–178.

Tully, James, "Le fédéralisme à voies multiples et la Charte", in Alain-G. Gagnon, ed., *Québec: État et société*, vol. 1, Montréal: Québec Amérique, 1994b, pp. 125–149.

Tully, James, "Multirow federalism and the Charter", in Philip Bryden, Steven Davis and John Russell, eds, *Protecting Rights and Freedoms: Essays on the Charter's Place in Canada's Political, Legal and Intellectual Life*, Toronto: University of Toronto Press, 1994c, pp. 178–204.

Tully, James, "Let's Talk: the Quebec Referendum and the Future of Canada", Austin and Hempel Lectures, Dalhousie University and University of Prince Edward Island, 23 and 27 March 1995a.

Tully, James, *Strange Multiplicity: Constitutionalism in an Age of Diversity*, Cambridge: Cambridge University Press, 1995b.

Tully, James, "Liberté et dévoilement dans les sociétés multinationales", *Globe: Revue internationale d'études québécoises*, 2, 2, 1999, pp. 13–36.

Tully, James, "The Unattained Yet Attainable Democracy: Canada and Quebec Face the New Century", *Les Grandes Conférences Desjardins*, Québec Studies Programme, McGill University, 23 March 2000.

Tully, James, "Introduction", in Alain-G. Gagnon and James Tully, *Multi-*

national Democracies, Cambridge: Cambridge University Press, 2001, pp. 1–33.

Turgeon, Luc, "La grande absente. La société civile au sein de la Révolution tranquille", *Globe: Revue internationale d'études québécoises*, 2, 1, 1999, pp. 35–56.

Turp, Daniel, *La nation bâillonnée. Le plan ou l'offensive d'Ottawa contre le Québec*, Montréal: VLB Éditeur, 2000.

Venne, Michel, ed., *Penser la nation québécoise*, Montréal: Québec Amérique, "Débats" collection, 2000.

Vernon, Richard, "The Federal Citizen", in M.W. Westmacott and R.D. Olling, eds, *Perspectives on Canadian Federalism*, Scarborough: Prentice-Hall Canada, 1988, pp. 3–15.

Vilar, Pierre, *Histoire de l'Espagne*, 1st edition, Paris: Les Presses Universitaires de France, 1947.

Vilar, Pierre, *La Catalogne dans l'Espagne moderne*, Paris: Flammarion, 1977.

Vipond, Robert, "From Provincial Autonomy to Provincial Equality (Or Clyde Wells and the Distinct Society)", in Joseph Carens, ed., *Is Quebec Nationalism Just? Perspectives from Anglophone Canada*, Montréal and Kingston: McGill-Queen's University Press, 1995, pp. 97–119.

Watts, Ronald L., *Executive Federalism: a Comparative Analysis*, Kingston: Institute of Intergovernmental Relations, Queen's University, 1989.

Watts, Ronald L., "Federalism and Diversity in Canada", in Yash Ghai, ed., *Autonomy and Ethnicity: Negotitating Claims in Multi-Ethnic States*, Cambridge: Cambridge University Press, 2000, pp. 29–52.

Watts, Ronald L., *Comparaison des régimes fédéraux*, 2nd edition, Kingston: Institut des relations intergouvernementales, 2002.

Webber, Jeremy, *Reimagining Canada: Language, Culture and the Canadian Constitution*, Montréal and Kingston: McGill-Queen's University Press, 1994.

Weiss, Linda, "Is the State Being Transformed by Globalisation?", in Linda Weiss, ed., *States in the Global Economy*, Cambridge: Cambridge University Press, 2003, pp. 293–317.

Wells, Paul, "Quebecers? Canadians? We're Proud to Be Both", *The Gazette*, 4 April 1998.

Wheare, Kenneth C., *Federal Government*, 4th edition, Oxford: Oxford University Press, 1967.

Whitaker, Reginald, *A Sovereign Idea: Essays on Canada as a Democratic Community*, Montreal: McGill-Queen's University Press, 1992.

Whitaker, Reginald, "The Dog that Never Barked: Who Killed Asymmetrical Federalism?", in Kenneth McRoberts and Patrick Monahan, eds, *The Charlottetown Accord, the Referendum, and the Future of Canada*, Toronto: University of Toronto Press, 1993, pp. 107–114.

White, Graham, "Treaty Federalism in Northern Canada: Aboriginal–Government Land Claims Boards", in *Publius*, 32, 3, summer 2002, pp. 89–114.

Wynn, Graeme, "Aux confins de l'empire 1760–1840", in Craig Brown and Paul-André Linteau, eds, *Histoire générale du Canada*, Montréal: Éditions du Boréal, 1990, pp. 223–332.

Young, Iris Marion, *Justice and the Politics of Difference*, Princeton: Princeton University Press, 1990.

Yuval-Davis, Nira, "Theorizing Gender and Nation", in Nira Yuval-Davis, ed., *Gender and Nation*, London: Sage, 1997, pp. 1–25.

Zapata-Barrero, Ricard, *Multiculturalidad e inmigracion*, Madrid: Editorial Syntesis, 2004.

Index

Printed in the United States
by Baker & Taylor Publisher Services